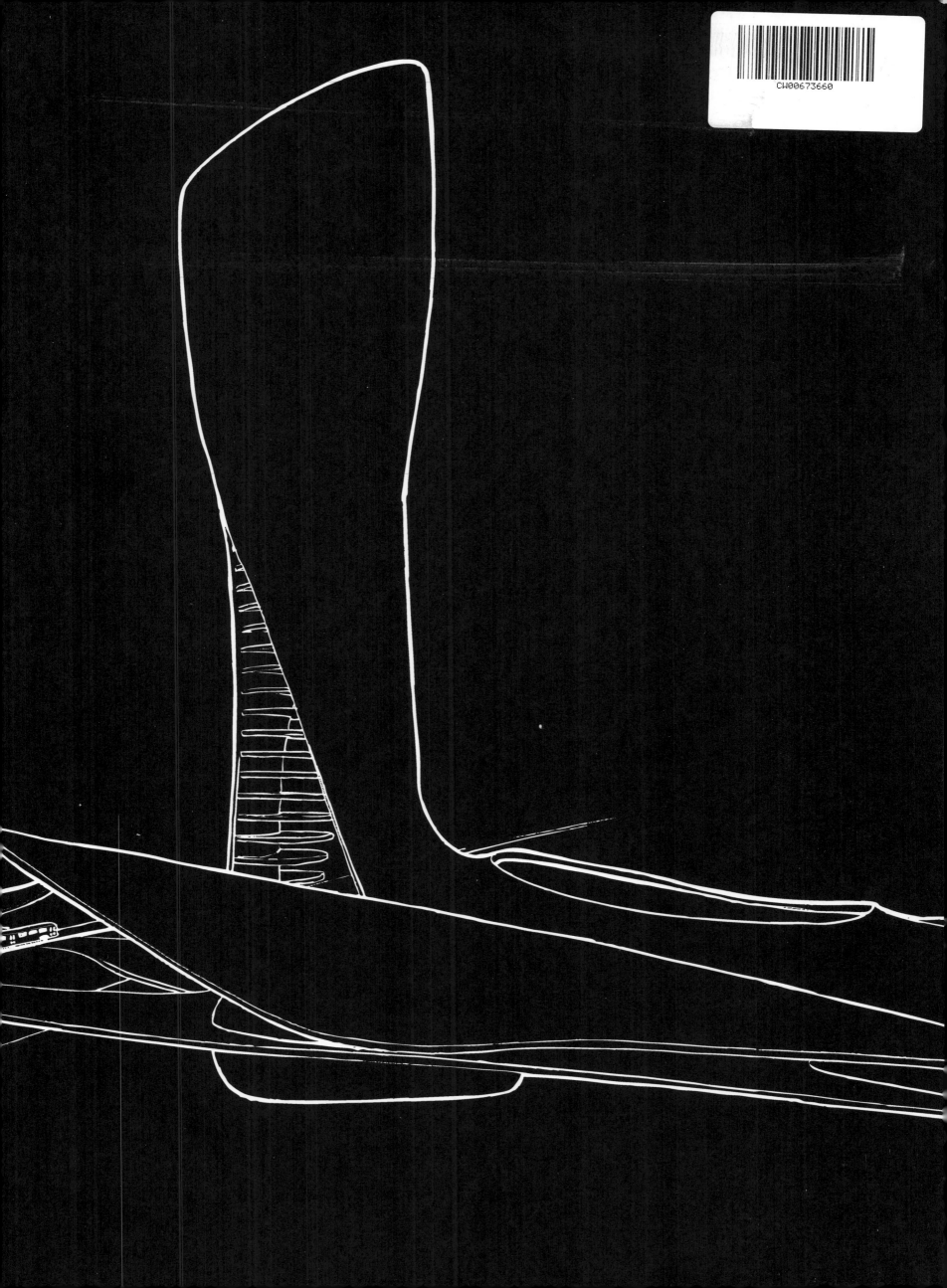

NEW FRONTIERS IN ARCHITECTURE

WHITE STAR PUBLISHERS

ARCHITECTURE
emirates between vision and reality

text
oscar eugenio bellini
laura daglio

project editor
valeria manferto de fabianis

editorial coordination
federica romagnoli

graphic design
maria cucchi

1 *Illustration of the Apeiron Island Hotel in Dubai, designed by Sybarite, London.*

2-3 *The skyline over Sheikh Zayed Road in Dubai.*

4-5 *The plan for the Performing Arts Centre on Saadiyat Island, Abu Dhabi.*

6-7 *The entrance to one of the two Emirates Towers, Dubai.*

8-9 *The Burj Al Arab on the left is the icon for Dubai's new urban development.*

CONTENTS

10 Abu Dhabi has begun a development on Saadiyat Island based on the allure of attractive buildings designed by large international firms intended to accommodate cultural spaces, exhibitions, and museums, in this case the Maritime Museum conceived by Tadao Ando.

11 The success of the construction boom in the United Arab Emirates is due in large part to the creation of an architectural utopia, which allows the limits of construction technology to be challenged without any financial regard. The Rotating Tower, a skyscraper whose floors rotate independently around a central vertical axis, is just one example.

INTRODUCTION

THE UNITED ARAB EMIRATES IS A
FEDERATION OF SEVEN STATES – ABU DHABI,
AJMAN, DUBAI, FUJAIRAH, SHARJAH, UMM
AL-QUAWAIN, AND RAS AL-KHAIMAH – WHICH
WAS FORMED BETWEEN 1971 AND 1972.
HOWEVER, WITHIN THE FEDERATION EACH
EMIRATE CONTINUES TO ENJOY GREAT
POLITICAL, JUDICIAL, AND ECONOMIC
AUTONOMY.

With an average altitude of less than 500
ft (152 m), the region is almost entirely
covered by a low-lying sandy desert dotted
with huge salt flats, with the exception of the
Al-Hajar mountain range on the border with
Oman. The most important cities, including
the administrative capital Abu Dhabi and the
business capital Dubai, are located along the
rugged coast of the Persian Gulf,
characterized by its extremely shallow waters
and numerous islands.

The area was settled in the Stone Age,
when the region was very different than it is
today. It was an important trade hub
between East and West from ancient times
until the 15th century, when the first
Europeans arrived. The Pirate Coast, as it
was known to travelers, was largely forgotten
until 1853, when it became a British
protectorate, which it remained until the
proclamation of the federation. At the end of
the 1960s, the discovery of extensive oil and
natural gas reserves heralded a new
economic era. However, it is estimated that
these reserves will run dry within a few years.

*12-13 This collage was designed by the OMA
Studio to compare the Dubai Renaissance design
(in the middle) with other skyscrapers throughout
the world and provides an interesting and varied
panorama of contemporary architecture.*

THE UNITED ARAB EMIRATES BETWEEN VISION AND REALITY

INTRODUCTION

Driven by the awareness of the inevitable exhaustion of their natural reserves, over the past few decades the emirates have drawn up a far-reaching development strategy aimed at the diversification of the economy with the creation of new service industries associated with finance, tourism, and leisure. The aim is to attract increasing flows of foreign capital and match the quality of living standards enjoyed by the most advanced nations. This has inevitably led to unprecedented urban growth, which in turn has spawned a massive building boom, with huge-scale construction projects of residential buildings, infrastructure, large hotels, shopping malls, sports and cultural facilities, office towers, and awesome "citadels" dedicated to leisure and entertainment.

Today, cities such as Dubai and Abu Dhabi are a unique blend of modernity and the timeless desert, where East and West merge. Not only are they experiencing extremely rapid urban development, but they also have some of the world's highest property incomes. Until recently the UAE was associated only with oil wells, but today it is seen as a desriable destination where every luxury can be enjoyed against a backdrop of sand dunes, sun, and sea, with daring, innovative skyscrapers, both commercial and residential, designed by some of the world's leading architecture firms. The Burj Al Arab is the symbol of this transformation. The speed at which this urban development has occurred, which has already created a huge

metropolitan area, and the lack of constraints on the radical and revolutionary architecture have been truly startling.

Desert landscapes have been transformed in a matter of a few years into expanses of skyscrapers and the pace of this rapid development has not slackened; nowhere more so than in Dubai, which as recently as the mid-1990s was still largely desert. This book can only offer a snapshot of such a rapidly changing landscape, because the process continues with the construction of buildings and other structures representing increasingly advanced technological achievements and establishing new and hitherto unthinkable thresholds of the possible. The property developers have found a way of publicizing themselves on an international scale through the creation of record-breaking buildings or projects that make headlines all over the world. Such developments are also record-breaking in terms of the billions of dollars being invested to finance this explosion of construction.

The UAE's flourishing economy is both a result of this development and one of the catalysts of the structural changes that, following 9/11, have led to the reinvestment within the country of the revenue derived from the oil industry, generating great wealth. The UAE, which appears to the world as an evolving economic rather than political power, is preparing to become the preferred business partner of the growing Asian market.

The country continues to challenge the rest of the world for the various records in

the construction sector, though both the designers and technologies have hitherto always come from abroad. This exciting environment has allowed the expression of the most audacious architectural designs. However, the concept of the skyscraper – freed from its role as a symbol of late 20th-century American power – continues to appeal mainly to property developers. However, the absence of restraints can also pose ethical and cultural problems. On the one hand, it is possible to object to the excess of luxury, of unrestrained consumption, or the working conditions of the laborers engaged in the building boom, while on the other hand an almost complete lack of urban planning and coordinated references and themes has led to a bewildering proliferation of styles. Environmental sustainability has also become a factor in the architectural experimentation, although the concept of environment – judging by the appearance of new artificial archipelagos – is not yet totally understood. It does appear that the individual governments are taking steps to regulate energy consumption in buildings: Dubai aims to cut its consumption by 60 per cent in relation to traditional cities.

This book aims to present as exhaustive an overview as possible of the latest architecture in the UAE, divided into functional types, in order to fully represent the extraordinary variety of solutions and experiments currently being constructed or proposed.   O.E.B. and L.D.

15 The more audcaiously ambitious the design, the greater the recognition in the local and international construction world. As one of the tallest residential skyscrapers in the world, the Pentominium is such audacious building.

16-17 The majority of the world's most renowned architecture firms and practices, such as the British-Iraqi Zaha Hadid, are involved in all the new developments planned for the United Arab Emirates. The UAE has become an exciting "architectural laboratory."

18-19 New architecture has design solutions that are both experimental and innovative, often involving original spatial solutions, such as in the atrium entrance to the Abu Dhabi Investment Authority.

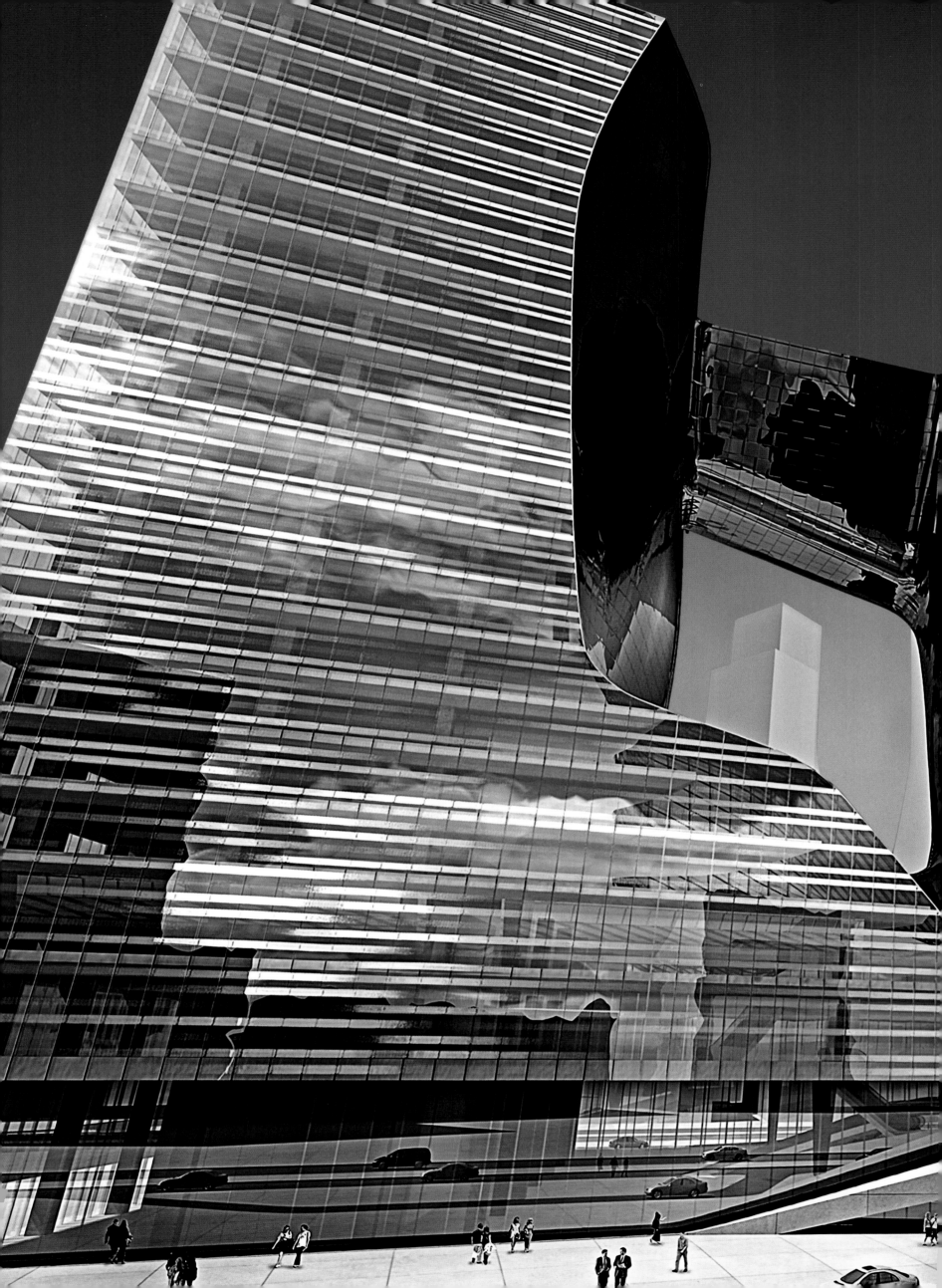

atkins & partners (21st century to

tower atedas ltd ocean he

skidmore, owings & merrill ll

rchitects (sa (me dubai) – dynamic

residential buildings

residential buildings

In the large new metropolitan area that is currently transforming the southeast coast of the Persian Gulf, residential architecture is assuming a prominent role in terms of property development and image, in addition to constituting a profitable form of investment. The end users of the residential towers are involved in the emergent holiday homes industry. The residential market is an international attraction not only for large real-estate companies, but also for small investors, as the region's breathtaking pace of expansion and transformation allows rapid and substantial returns. Growth is both self-sustaining and boosted by a global media campaign that promotes facilities and creates tourist attractions through a series of projects in all possible sectors, ranging from sport to leisure and culture. In this context residential building transcends the mere function of housing to become an authentic consumer product, which is therefore based on several factors – primarily artificially induced needs – and always within a framework characterized by fierce competition. Prestige and exclusiveness are the keywords and dominant factors that drive the construction sector and constitute its main attraction, and their pursuit is not limited by either technological or economic considerations, for guaranteed returns are assured on even the most daring projects. In the case of residential towers (but also commercial buildings), luxury has always been the primary factor on which the race for entrepreneurial success has been based; and luxury has always been identified with economic power and prestige.

The quality of the fittings and materials of both the apartments and the public areas exudes extravagant wealth, which is immediately expressed in the entrance halls.

Luxury also signifies the opportunity to choose and customize the apartments' interiors with furnishings in the most diverse styles, from classic to minimalist modern. The bathrooms and kitchens are the best available on the international market, and whirlpool tubs have become a standard accessory, overshadowed by the exciting new possibility of small private swimming pools, as featured in several projects. The state-of-the-art plant uses the most sophisticated domotic (building automation) systems and offers total control of the indoor climate, even allowing residents to choose the most appropriate lighting and background music for every moment. In short, the apartments increasingly resemble the exclusive suites of the city's most prestigious hotels, including services, which have become essential for these residential buildings.

Residents not only have dedicated staff and concierge services at their disposal, but can enjoy wellness facilities, such as gyms and spas, sunbathe around outdoor swimming pools and on terraces, conduct business in lobbies furnished with IT equipment and meeting tables, and even entertain guests in lounges or ballrooms.

The most emblematic example of a building with such facilities is undoubtedly the Pentominium in Dubai, which even offers residents access to a fleet of prestigious cars and pleasure craft. As in the luxury hotels, the services are housed on the lower floors and the commercial areas on the intermediate ones or on the roof, thus allowing breathtaking views. Indeed, another factor in the development and evolution of these residential towers is the desire for the widest possible panormaic views. This requires the construction of ever-taller towers, which combine the potential for spectacular views with the prestige of living in a record-breaking building.

The most exclusive residential units – and also the most important ones from an economic viewpoint – are undoubtedly the penthouses, which are even more luxurious in terms of size and layout, arranged on two or even three floors, where refinement has reached hitherto unknown levels. The unbroken façades of these buildings are not simply a formal stylistic solution, but allow spectacular floor-to-ceiling panoramic views. In the case of 55° Time and the Rotating Tower, the quest for this particular added value has resulted in amazing structures – an entire tower in the case of the former and individual floors in the latter – that revolve around a central axis in order to ensure 360-degree views over the surrounding areas. In other cases (for example, the Empire Tower and Ocean Heights) the shapes of the buildings are sculpted, inclined, and rotated to create a static form that maximizes sea vistas for the largest possible number of residential units. Views over the Persian Gulf, or at least over the water, also increase the value of property, heavily influencing the planning of new districts. In residential towers, the work of the designer concentrates more on the interiors, aiming for luxury, spectacular views, and services, than the quest for iconic status that characterizes public, commercial, and hotel buildings. While in these cases buildings are conceived as unique landmarks, strongly affecting their composition and shapes, residential towers are, with rare exceptions, designed in a style aimed at conveying their formal identity.   L.D.

24 The treatment of the main façade is characterized by the stylized image of a gigantic wing, created with silver foil panels and accented by the calligraphic, horizontal "strokes" of glass.

25 The rounded corner of the building at the intersection of Sheikh Zayed Road and another cross street follows the specific shape of the lot on which it is built to take the maximum advantage of available space.

21st Century Tower

DUBAI

Upon its completion in 2003, the 21st Century Tower was the world's tallest residential tower (883 ft/269 m) until the construction of the Q1 tower on Australia's Gold Coast (1,058 ft/322 m) in 2005, which has subsequently also been overtaken by other buildings. The temporary height record was achieved by the distinctive turret supporting a spire, which together rise almost 100 ft (30 m) above the height of the actual roof.

The tower is one of the many skyscrapers that line Dubai's famous Sheikh Zayed Road. In a stretch of just over a mile more than 25 buildings taller than 328 ft (100 m) have been constructed in the space of a few years, with the explicit intention of emulating Manhattan or Chicago's Magnificent Mile. Several of these were designed by WS Atkins and Partners, which was also responsible for the architectural and engineering design of the 21st Century Tower and its interiors and oversaw the construction of the project. Atkins is the largest engineering consultancy in the United Kingdom and one of the largest global design firms, in terms of both size (17,000 employees in 60 branches all over the world) and expertise. In this case the need to make full use of the site (a rectangular plot with one corner cut off by a highway) suggested the design of the structure,

characterized by two intersecting volumes: a cylinder, made from glass, standing on the missing part of the plot, and a parallelepiped. They are connected by a curved vertical element resembling a wing, whose tip rises above the cylindrical volume and forms the base of the spire. The symbolism of the feathered wing is further emphasized by the pattern of horizontal lines on the panels cladding the structure, which alternate white steel and blue glass.

The concept of flight is echoed in the image of the three overlapping doves affixed to the turret, which is the logo of the Al Rostamani Group, the property's developer. It is also indirectly evoked by the building's inhabitants, because the 400 luxurious one- and two-room apartments, with a combined area of over 760,000 sq ft (70,000 sq m) arranged on 50 floors, are rented to the crew members of Emirates Airline, who can enjoy facilities such as a retail floor at the entrance, a gym on the top floor, a rooftop pool, and 412 parking spaces in the adjoining nine-story building.

The maintenance and service rooms are distributed on various floors and the multistory parking lot features state-of-the-art cooling systems allowing the efficient air-conditioning of the tower despite the torrid climate.

26 left The prestigious glass entrance to this building on Sheikh Zayed Road is protected and shaded by a projecting roof made of stainless-steel sheet metal and flanked by columns covered with the same material.

26 right The opposite side of this building on Sheikh Zayed Road is simpler and more symmetrical, incorporating aluminum panels that frame the building's fluid façade of blue glass and emphasizing its balanced geometry.

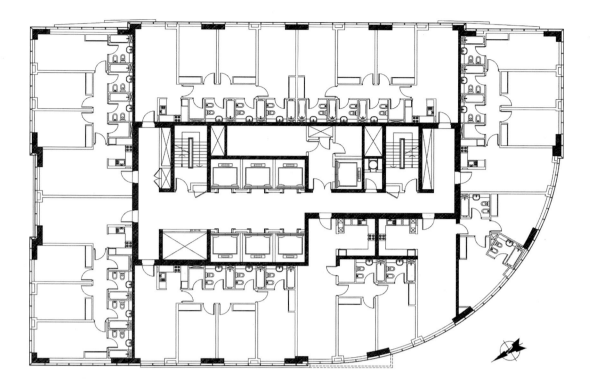

The residential units are arranged around a central core housing stairs and elevators, which form the skyscraper's reinforced concrete structural frame together with a series of pillars around the perimeter. In keeping with the client's requests, high-quality materials were used in the construction of the tower – the entrance is entirely clad with Carrara marble – whose durable and hard-wearing qualities will preserve its good looks over time.

The prestige of the apartments overlooking the Persian Gulf or Sheikh Zayed Road is heightened by the extensive views that are the main attraction of skyscraper living, although oddly the tower has no balconies. While the building was initially planned for mixed use, the office space was subsequently entirely converted to residential use.   L.D.

27 top These apartments, which are used by Emirates Airlines personnel, are arranged around a central core of vertical connections with non-load-bearing walls in reinforced concrete.

27 bottom This drawing depicts the vertical section of the lobby and illustrates the materials used as interior surface finishes, among which Carraran white marble and stainless steel predominate.

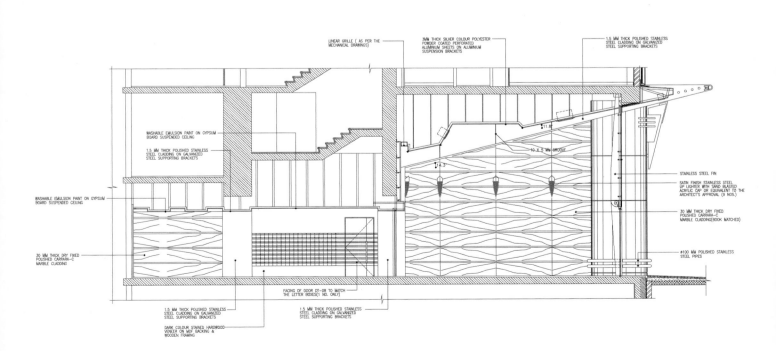

Chelsea Tower

DUBAI

W S A T K I N S & P A R T N E R S

The Chelsea Tower stands out from the anonymous uniformity of the skyscrapers lining Dubai's famous Sheikh Zayed Road not so much for its height of 820 ft (250 m), but for its unique design, as explicitly requested by the client. The building is characterized by a diagonal spine that cuts across its practically rhomboid plan, with two tall pilasters at the corners that meet high above the roof, creating a window that frames the sky.

The structure's simple composition is attentively styled, as though it were a sleek design object. The faces of the service levels are set back, grouping the residential floors into three identical blocks, whose slightly curved façades create a dynamic effect. Balconies of different lengths extend from the two huge angular uprights of the spine, which are lightened by vertical slits running to the top of the building, creating an alternating pattern of horizontal lines that seem to support the curtain walls of the residential units. This decorative solution is emphasized by the color contrast created by the cobalt blue glass against the white aluminum panels that clad the corner elements and the parapets. A slender needle-like spire is suspended in the middle of the diagonal frame, where it meets above the tower's roof, underscoring the two symmetrical axes of the building's plan and distinguishing it from the surrounding structures. The tower's design has given it an iconic status and a captivating image, emphasizing its uniqueness in a constantly changing urban landscape.

Inside the tower a square central core made from reinforced concrete houses the stairs and elevators and performs a structural function; its sides are continued outward in a swastika arrangement that stiffens the structure. The residential units are partly contained in the diagonal spine, whose load-bearing function is limited to two large inner pillars on the corners. The 278 serviced apartments, with one, two or three bedrooms, offer guests business services on the ground floor and sports facilities, including an 82-ft (25-m) swimming pool, a gym, and squash courts on the roof of the adjoining 347-space multistory parking lot.

Like many other buildings in Dubai, the Chelsea Tower (completed in 2005) was designed by WS Atkins & Partners, which was one of the first architecture firms to update the formal language of these structures and to give them greater prestige and visibility, combined with luxurious finishes and interiors. Several aspects, such as the choice of materials and the horizontal divisions, are reminiscent of the 21st Century Tower, which stands opposite the building on the other side of the highway. Atkins' Dubai branch oversaw the project, from its inception to the detailed definition of the various architectural, structural and engineering aspects, and coordinated its construction.   L.D.

28 The original design of this building plays on the chromatic contrast between white and blue, reflecting the design brief that requested a strong image with features that would distinguish it within the city skyline.

29 The top of this skyscraper is characterized by a large square element created by joining two angled pilasters, which then frame the sky and whose center line couples with the central pinnacle.

Chelsea Tower

30 top The main building is connected to a nearby parking structure by a pedestrian walkway with a transparent cover in circular sections as seen here from the interior.

30 bottom The 82-ft (25-m) long outdoor pool is part of the many facilities available in the sports complex that has been constructed on the roof of the building's own parking lot.

31 Both designed by WS Atkins & Partners, this photograph shows a stretch of Sheikh Zayed Road where the Chelsea Tower, above left, and the 21st Century Tower, below right, are easily recognized.

MARINA HEIGHTS TOWER مارينا هايتس تاور

32-33 The façades of this skyscraper are covered with prefabricated concrete and glass panels. Shown here is the entrance to the tower that rises up from a quadrangular base whose space can be seen from two sides.

33 The main façade of this building is turned towards the Dubai Marina's canal, one of the largest ever constructed. Its banks have equipment and berths for numerous pleasure craft.

Marina Heights Tower

DUBAI

The residential Marina Heights Tower, completed in 2006, is one of an array of skyscrapers that will line the waterfront of Dubai Marina, the world's largest artificial marina. The area, whose attraction to developers lies in the many waterfront sites created by the excavation of the new marina, lies between the coast and Sheikh Zayed Road, making it easily accessible from the rest of the city. Marina Heights Tower was designed by the architectural practice RMJM, based in Britain but with branches worldwide, which was responsible for both the structural and engineering aspects of the project, and oversaw its construction.

A four-sided podium with five floors forms the base of the actual tower, which is in the shape of a prism with an elongated hexagonal base. Standing 682 ft (207 m) tall, the structure's main façades are divided into three parts. Indeed, the geometric design of the cladding panels and glass changes above the 30th floor, which houses an open terrace, while the upper part of the building is set back from the lower floors.

Marina Heights Tower

The side façades, protected from the sun and the wind by prefabricated brises-soleils, are uniform to the base of the crown. The surface of the helipad is bent slightly upward, like two wings, and rests on the crown, reinforcing the vaguely Orientalizing appearance of the building and its design.

Unlike the tower, where the focus is on the symmetry of the façades, the design of the exterior of the podium is freer and more variable, also due to the sliding wooden screens of the residential terraces.

The 55-story Marina Heights Tower, conceived to provide its residents with a high standard of living, offers a wide variety of apartments with one, two, three, four and five bedrooms, as well as duplex units on the upper floors and two penthouses with views on three sides. The interiors have open floor plans with few internal walls, allowing greater flexibility and a more fluid perception of space. The decor can be personalized with styles ranging from Classic, with natural wood and marble, to the more minimalist Contemporary, featuring stainless steel, and Prestige, with richer, more sophisticated materials and fixtures. The building also has facilities such as stores on the ground floor, a business center for residents, a large parking lot, and accommodation for service staff.   L.D.

34-35 The base of this building is excavated to emphasize the three-floor high entrance of this residential skyscraper, covered in stone and finished with ample glass surfaces and stainless steel features.

Ocean Heights

DUBAI

DAMAC Ocean Heights is an 82-story residential tower that will be situated in the Dubai Marina development near the Palm Jumeirah. This prestigious site influenced the design of the tower, which was developed with the aim of ensuring sea views for all the apartments, including those on the opposite side, thus maximizing the property's real-estate value. Three of the building's façades will rise twisting from the four-sided base, rising above the neighboring buildings from the 50th floor. As it reaches upward, the tower's floor areas are reduced in size, which will make the rotation more pronounced and give the elegant structure an even more slender appearance. The building breaks away from the orthogonal grid as it rises, and will assume the form of a growing plant organism. This dynamic design contrasts with the functional layout of the residential units, which will be arranged in a manner that will enhance their marketability.

Aedas, the international firm that designed the project for DAMAC Properties, devised a 13-ft (4-m) module that is repeated on each floor and changing only on the façade. This innovation also simplified the structural system. Shear walls stand either side of the central core housing the elevators and stairs, perpendicular to the mean of the two most extreme angles of the façade; an expedient aimed at minimizing the irregularity of the floor plans. In addition to the tower's amenities, which include a swimming pool, gym, sauna and hammam, and children's play area, owners of the 672 one-, two- and three-bedroom apartments will also enjoy the wide range of facilities available in the surrounding area, such as shopping arcades, a golf course, and luxury beaches. L.D.

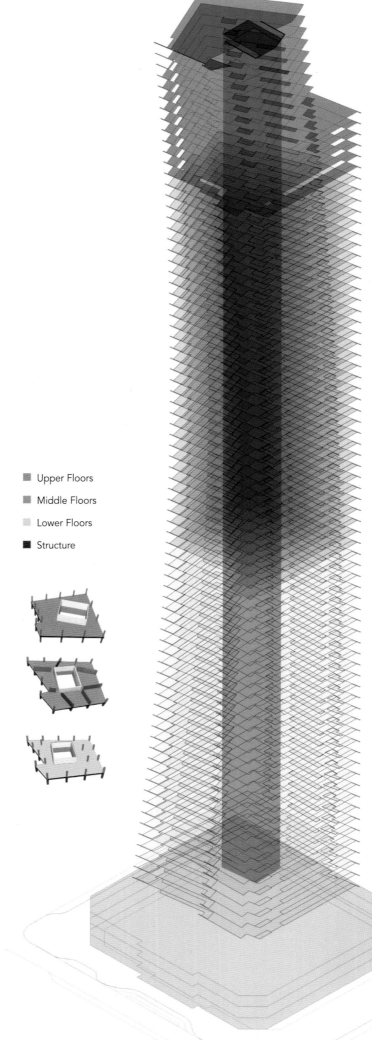

- Upper Floors
- Middle Floors
- Lower Floors
- Structure

36 Although the volume twists and opens as it rises, this blueprint shows how the structural system is based upon a strictly regular module, which tracks its way down through all the building's floors.

37 Positioned on a coastal lot near Dubai Marina, this tower was designed in such a way as to maximize panoramic views towards the Persian Gulf by inclining three sides of its base.

Pentominium

DUBAI

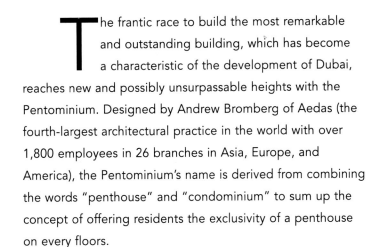

The frantic race to build the most remarkable and outstanding building, which has become a characteristic of the development of Dubai, reaches new and possibly unsurpassable heights with the Pentominium. Designed by Andrew Bromberg of Aedas (the fourth-largest architectural practice in the world with over 1,800 employees in 26 branches in Asia, Europe, and America), the Pentominium's name is derived from combining the words "penthouse" and "condominium" to sum up the concept of offering residents the exclusivity of a penthouse on every floors.

It is one of the world's tallest residential towers under construction (1,693 ft/516 m) and so will ensure breathtaking views over the Persian Gulf, the striking nearby Palm Jumeirah island, and the city. However, the primary aim of its developer, Trident International Holdings (who specialize in prestigious seafront homes), is to offer the most luxurious apartments in the world, with exceptionally large dimensions and superior quality, including superb services.

Each floor will house just one apartment (with an area of over 6,450 sq ft/600 sq m), boasting large balconies, four bedrooms (each with a large en suite bathroom), a double living area, divided into a family living room and a huge reception room, and accommodation for service staff. Access is through a private atrium served by elevators, while a biometric control system ensures maximum security. All the interiors are by the world-renowned designers HBA/Hirsch Bedner and Associates, whose long experience includes the decor of international hotel chains such as the Ritz Carlton, Grand Hyatt, and Four Seasons.

The upper floors will house a sky lounge, a swimming pool, a business center and an observatory, as well as separate health clubs for men and women, squash courts, a banquet hall, a private theater, and a cigar lounge. In keeping with such a prestigious residential tower, these facilities are luxuriously designed in order to gratify the senses and satisfy the whims of its future residents. The health centers will be run by Six Senses Spa, the world leader in the sector, all the accessories of the business center will be supplied by Tiffany, the cigar lounge stocked by Davidoff, the hi-fi and video equipment of the apartments will be from the top of Bang & Olufsen's product range, and the public areas will be decorated with Swarovski crystals.

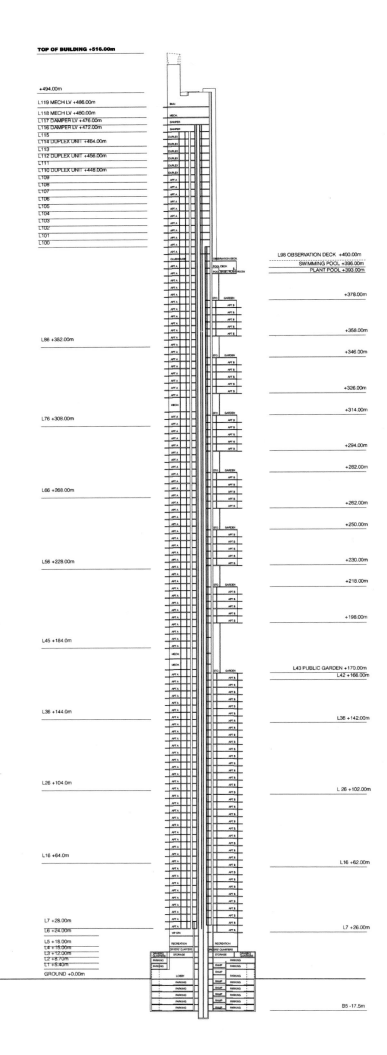

38 In the vertical section, you can easily see the open spaces characterizing the sawtooth profile of the northern portion of this building, and, on the right side of the drawing, the design for hanging gardens.

39 This view shows the south side of the tower characterized by a special transparent glass screen that enlarges the upper floors and protects the terraces from sun and wind.

Pentominium

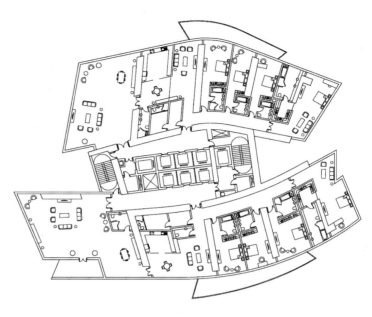

AEDAS LTD

The Quintessentially Club will provide a 24-hour concierge service to solve any problems and offer residents further privileges and exclusive benefits. A fleet of Rolls-Royces and Azimut motor yachts will also be available for residents.

In the rapidly expanding Dubai Marina, the tower's elegant, slim form will ensure that it stands out from the other buildings. The plan consists of two parts arranged around a central elevator core. The entire 120 floors of the southwest-facing building overlooking the sea will appear substantially regular and will be encased in a transparent curtain wall that will make the structure seem even more slender. The special glass panels from which it is made will have the dual function of shielding the building from excessive solar radiation and wind, particularly on the upper floors, which are more exposed to this problem, where they widen progressively to protect the open living areas of the balconies. The prism that will rise from the base on the opposite side will be interrupted by seven large five- or six-story spaces that lighten the composition. These voids will house hanging gardens and alternate with the regular solids of the inhabited floors to create the building's distinctive saw-toothed profile.   L.D.

40-41 *This building rises from the cityscape to a height of 1,693 ft (516 m). You can make out the profile of Jumeirah Palm Island, one of three artificial palm tree-shaped islands along the coast of Dubai.*

41 *This building's design highlights the two forms in its structure; each one occupied by one whole apartment and linked in the center through a nucleus of vertical connections.*

Empire Island Tower

ABU DHABI

The residential Empire Tower, designed by the international architecture firm Aedas, will be part of the urban development of the Shams area of Al Reem Island in Abu Dhabi. Empire Holdings, which commissioned the structure, explicitly requested a simple, linear building that would stand out from the elaborate forms of its neighbors. The proposed solution maximizes the views from the apartments on the various levels, with vistas of the island's Central Park on one side and the sea on the other. This is highly significant, for the financial viability of the project, which is dependent on presales within an extremely competitive market.

The volumetric composition of the building is characterized by several vertical layers of variable thickness that spread along the ground, following the property lines, before rising upwards and narrowing and then sloping slightly again. The highly dynamic effect of the 794-ft (242-m) tall building will offer the potential for vastly improved views towards the coast, for the tower's distinctive form will allow it to divert attention from a nearby skyscraper and direct it towards the sea.

Despite its stunning appearance, the building's design is actually very simple, featuring a glass curtain wall with balconies in the interstices of the vertical layers. The tower has a total floor area of approximately one million sq ft (92,000 sq m) arranged on 57 floors, with apartments with one to four bedrooms. Residents will be able to enjoy such amenities as an underground parking lot, a swimming pool, a sauna and whirlpool tubs, an outdoor public lounge, a garden, a gym and a rooftop helipad.   L.D.

42 In a three-dimensional simulation, the skyscraper's overall compositional theme, i.e. the juxtaposition of vertical inclined planes, is evident in its complexity and endows the whole structure with a remarkable dynamic stature.

43 left This vertical section clarifies the lines of the inclined floors and building's overall silhouette, emphasizing the relationship between vertical connections, common areas, and duplex and triplex apartments.

43 right These blueprints illustrate the integrated form of the skyscraper with its adjacent parallelepiped spaces, broken up by vertical planes that incline and enlarge the spaces.

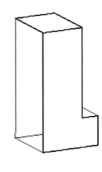

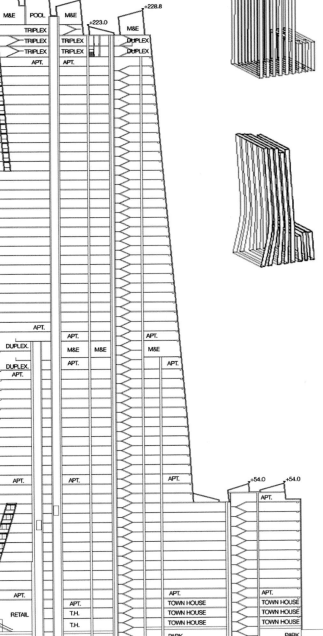

Al Sharq Tower

DUBAI

44 left The tower's façade highlights its extremely narrow shape produced through a 1:10 ratio between the foundation and the height of the façade. A parking lot is connected to the building, with space for about 800 vehicles.

44 right This blueprint demonstrates the circular foundations of the eight cylinders comprising this building, with its core of vertical connections in the center.

45 In a night-time view, this 3D simulation demonstrates the spatial volume of this skyscraper consisting of eight side-by-side cylinders. The building's configuration is a brilliant and evocative symbol within the urban context.

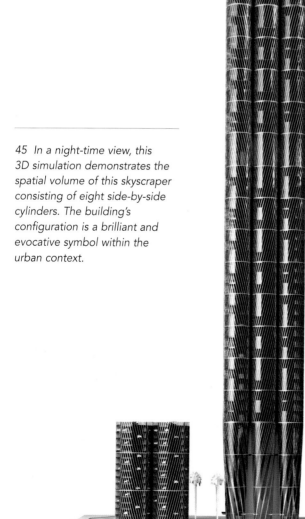

The Al Sharq Tower is part of a larger scheme by the Dubai-based property development company Al Sharq Investment, involving the construction of six new projects throughout Dubai, including commercial buildings, offices, and a water park, costing a total of over a billion U.S. dollars. At 1,181 ft (360 m) high, the tower is intended to be the tallest skyscraper on Sheikh Zayed Road in the heart of the city's financial and business district. The famous architecture firm Skidmore, Owings and Merrill LLP (SOM) are responsible for both its design and engineering.

The tower will have 100 residential floors, with ceiling heights ranging from 11 to 23 ft (3 to 7m), and two service areas situated above the 82-ft (25-ft) high lobby and on the upper floors. It will boast a wellness center, a gym, swimming pools, party rooms, a projection room, play areas, and restaurants, including a revolving one on the roof. The spaces destined for the residential units are all located at a height of at least 130 ft (40 m) above the ground, in order to ensure prestigious views over the city.

A simple, modular configuration was chosen for the building. The square plan contains nine circles arranged in three rows of three, which rise to form cylinders, each with a diameter of 40 ft (12 m).

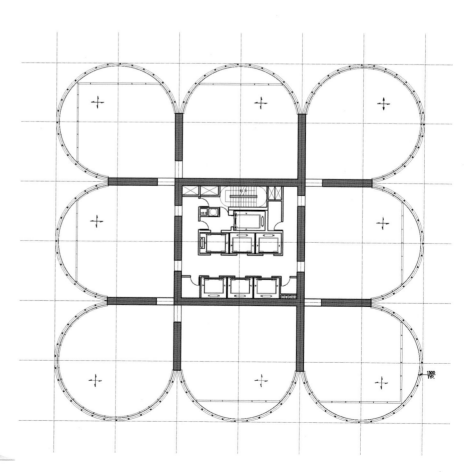

This bundle of tubes will appear extremely slender, due to the 1:10 ratio between the building's width and total height, giving it both formal purity and an extremely sleek appearance. The structural framework is comprised of four reinforced concrete shear walls, whose thickness will taper from 50 inches (1.27 m) at the base to 23 inches (58 cm) at the upper levels. They will be arranged in a shape resembling a tic-tac-toe board, the central section of which will house elevator shafts and stairwells. The prestressed concrete floor plates will be 8 inches (20 cm) thick. Galvanized steel wire with a diameter varying from 0.6 to 2 inches (1.5–6 cm) will be used to strengthen the entire structure. Spaced 60 inches (1.52 m) apart and anchored back to the shear walls that extend between each tube, the cables will be wrapped around the completely glazed skin of each cylinder, forming a spiral pattern that will give the structure a sense of dynamism. This effect will be accentuated during the day due to the iridescent effect of reflected light, while the transparent building will become a luminous landmark at night.

The building's 268 luxurious apartments will be in the adjoining circular spaces of the plan and boast large living areas, column-free interiors, and loggias created by setting back the perpendicular glazed walls from the curved perimeter wrapped in the spiraling cables. The state-of-the-art mechanical and electrical systems will be housed on three levels. An 800-vehicle parking lot will be in a building adjoining the tower and will feature a highly automated system, allowing cars to be parked on mobile platforms on the ground, which are then raised and moved horizontally to the designated spaces by a computerized system, offering residents an exclusive service and greater security.   L.D.

46 top The distinctive feature of the glass façades are the steel cables that wrap each cylinder with a spiral to strengthen the structure.

46 bottom These apartments with modern interior surface finishes and furnishings enjoy completely glassed-in floor-to-ceiling views, unobstructed by any other vertical structures.

47 A striking night-time simulation highlights the cross-stitched steel cabling that spirals around the building in full view from the ground-floor lobby.

55° Time Dubai

DUBAI

Following its completion, 55° Time will be the first of 24 prestigious and environmentally sustainable residential buildings to be built in the world's leading cities. All will be named after their longitude, but their most amazing aspect is that they will slowly rotate in synchrony around their vertical axes to offer 360-degree views. This daring design offers an innovative solution to the problem of providing a comprehensive view of a building's surroundings for all the residents – a powerful commercial advantage. The panorama that may be admired from the Dubai pilot project's seamless glazed walls is that of the City of Arabia, one of the themed zones of Dubailand, which is an enormous new development covering an area of almost 12 sq miles (31 sq km). Dubailand is intended to make Dubai the leading tourist destination in the Middle East, with amusement parks of all kinds and enormous sports areas and shopping malls to satisfy the requirements of visitors from all over the world.

In this first project, solar energy is used to power the tower's rotation, which moves through an angle of approximately 52 degrees per day, at a speed of 2.07 ft (63 cm) per minute, completing the cycle in a week. The mechanism, designed by Nick Cooper of British engineering company M.G. Bennett & Associates, already famous for moving large structures, reduces the effective mass of the building from 88,000 to 11,000 tons (80,000 to 9,900 tonnes). The building will revolve by means of 20 electric motors mounted on a system of ball bearings with an overall diameter of 98 ft (29 m) coated with a special polymer to reduce friction. At the base a line will mark the time of day as the structure revolves, allowing it to act as a huge and very expensive timepiece.

48 The most prestigious three-level apartments have 23-ft (7-m) built-in private pools on the top floor connected to personal gyms with spectacular exterior panoramic views.

49 This skyscraper is characterized by a two-layer glass enclosure that enwraps the building to roof level, then it emerges as a spiral profile.

A crescent-shaped element is mounted at the top of the structure.

50-51 These triplex apartments have living rooms with cathedral ceilings and second-floor personal fitness rooms overlooking them. A 20-ft (6-m) high sculpture accents the wall in the background.

55° Time Dubai

The architectural design represents the first large international project outside Europe by the British firm Glenn Howells Architects and is very simple. The 30-story revolving tower will be positioned almost in the center of a 65-ft (20-m) tall square base and topped by a three-dimensional crescent. The tall cylindrical structure will be literally wrapped in a ventilated double-skinned wall that will be completely transparent from floor to ceiling, and will house the outer areas of the residential units on the upper floors, offering occupants better climate control with reduced energy costs. The wrapping effect of the skin, which will emphasize the tower's dynamism, will be accentuated by the inclination of the uprights of the frame, culminating in the spiral form of the crown. A theater and open-air observatory are planned for the roof, while the top floor will be home to a music room. Other facilities, including a daycare center and a gym, will be situated on the lower floors of the tower. A 200-ft (60-m) swimming pool, solarium, and a hanging garden will be on the roof of the base, which will house the movement mechanism and a lobby.

The residential units will be located in sections of the ring-shaped outer area of the tower, which will surround a central core housing elevator shafts and stairwells, and feature interesting design solutions and interiors. The floor plans are adjustable thanks to the use of sliding walls and are laid out on a single level with one or two bedrooms, on two levels with three or four bedrooms, or on three levels with double-height living rooms and a private swimming pool flush with the floor.   L.D.

52-53 The fitness area in these triplex apartments includes a gym, sauna, Turkish bath, and private pool. An open corner bar is equipped with a small wine cellar.

52 bottom These apartment interiors have a highly sophisticated design, incorporating a minimalist contemporary style based on white accented with steel and glass.

53 This 3D simulation represents the revolving tower in a night-time situation. Piercing light enveloping the cylindrical structure in a spiral creates a regal and dynamic effect.

Rotating Tower

DUBAI

While the introduction of the concept of time to architecture is not a new one, the Florence-based Israeli architect David Fisher offers a spectacularly intriguing interpretation of it in his Rotating Tower project, which has become the emblem of his personal city-planning philosophy of "Dynamic Architecture." This is a concept well suited to the stupendous buildings of Dubai, where the first Rotating Tower will be built before being replicated in a further 11 cities around the world. Fisher's concept focuses on several current trends, such as moving buildings in order to increase the views available from the inhabited spaces and the growing awareness of energy conservation.

This skyscraper, designed by Marco Sala and Fabio Bettazzi, features a central core housing elevator shafts and plant, around which each of the 68 stories can rotate independently.

54-55 This image of the Dubai Rotating Tower is not static but dynamic as the building takes on diverse configurations night and day due to the ability of each floor to rotate independently from the others.

55 This building offers many diverse and formal solutions guaranteed by the jagged profile of its rotating floors, which, according to their position, result in the changing contours of the tower.

Rotating Tower

Residents on the top five floors – each housing a single 16,000-sq-ft (1,500 sq m) penthouse, the uppermost one will have a rooftop pool, and all with parking on the same level accessed by a special elevator – will be able to select the direction and speed of rotation by voice-activated remote control. The other residential units, hotel suites, and offices will turn at a speed of two to three revolutions per hour programmed by the architect or building manager. The irregular, ragged shape of the tower, determined by the rotating rings of the different levels, will thus change constantly and unexpectedly to maximize natural lighting or simply to choose the view best suited to the resident's mood. Moreover, the structural design – in which high-rise engineer Leslie Robertson of New-York-based engineering firm LERA acted as consultant – is better able to withstand earthquakes, due to the rigidity of the structural core, and cyclones, as it can automatically adopt the form best suited to the dynamics of the individual meteorological event.

Now that the main technological obstacles have been overcome, economic cost would appear to pose the only limit to such bizarre architecture, even in similar cases of apparently bold property marketing. However, the rotating tower not only takes into consideration the cost of construction, but also running costs. In this respect, too, the solutions are not new only taken to extremes. Indeed, the skyscraper will be the first in the world to be 90 percent prefabricated. The reinforced central core will be the only part of the structure to be built on site. The entirely prefabricated modules, complete with systems and fixtures, in which the individual floors are arranged in 12 segments, will be installed automatically onto this core. The factory-based construction techniques (all the workshops are based in Dubai) will allow greater control over final quality and timing, require fewer onsite laborers (the number can be reduced from 2,000 to 90), and consequent higher safety in the workplace.

The building will not only be self-sufficient in energy terms, but it will also generate surplus electricity sufficient to supply a further 2,200 families. Indeed, from the tenth floor up, 84 vertical-axis wind turbines with carbon-fiber blades are partially hidden in the spaces between the stories, which it is estimated will be able to generate approximately 1.2 million kilowatt-hours per year on the basis of wind conditions in Dubai. The system has a shell to protect it from wind blowing in the opposite direction to rotation, ensuring the continuity of movement. However, the building will also feature solar cells arranged on the rooftops, offering another source of electricity. This innovative proposal has aroused the interest of large local companies and multinationals in the construction sector, which have signed up to participate in the project as partners. L.D.

56 From glassed-in interiors, one may enjoy a 360-degree panorama thanks to the slow rotation of each floor on the building's vertical axis.

57 top left The extreme freedom and unpredictability of its resulting configuration is the foundation of this stunning design by architect David Fisher – there are plans to build similar buildings in other cities.

57 bottom left The rotational process of the floors may be either automatic, as stipulated by conditions in the lease, or changed at any time by vocal commands from the tenant.

57 right The tower's changing spatial volume may vary with the movement and also according to the geometry of each rotating floor. The intention is to maximize views and also to provide natural light over the course of the day.

58 Single floors are composed of prefabricated modules complete with surface finishes that have been quickly mounted to the reinforced concrete central nucleus of elevators, staircases, and other vertical connections.

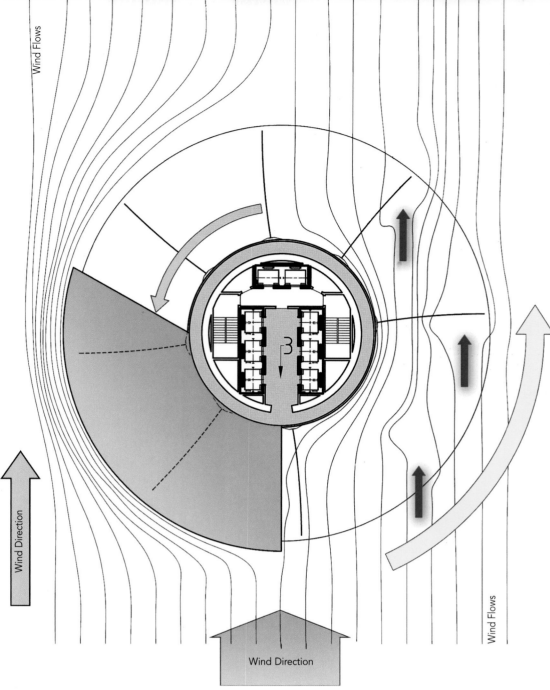

Wind Flows

Wind Direction

Wind Direction

Wind Flows

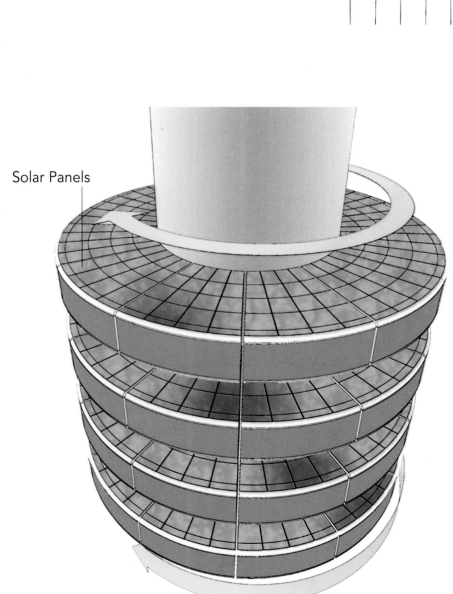

Solar Panels

59 top Horizontal wind turbines with carbon-fiber blades have been installed between rotating floors, protected by an external shell that prevents any adverse effect on their rotation from opposing winds.

59 bottom The drawing on the left shows the photovoltaic cells positioned between each rotating floor. The blueprint on the right demonstrates the vertical axonometric section of wind turbines rotating around the building's vertical axis.

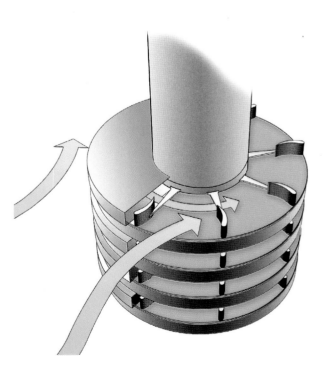

60 top This vertical section of the building shows each single floor separated over the height of the building to allow installation of wind turbines, the central core of vertical connections, and individual parking areas for each privately owned apartment.

60 bottom These luxurious villas on the upper levels are equipped with their very own private elevators specifically designed for the residents' cars. The elevators transport the vehicles directly to and from the chosen floor and the street.

60-61 In the floor plan layout of each prefabricated level, open walkways with cantilevered sections that independently rotate have been incorporated into the design, creating diverse configurations of form throughout the whole complex.

norr group consultants int. ltd.

dubai building) - carlos ott architec

gensler *(the gate)* - kohn pederse

authority tower) - jung brannen

engineers *(media 1 tower)* - ws atkir

architecture *(014)*

offices

carlos ott architect *(national bank of*
(national bank of abu dhabi headquarters) -
fox associates *(abu dhabi investment*
:sociates, dewan architects &
& partners *(sheth tower iris bay) -* rur

offices

During the 1980s and 1990s the UAE's economic strategy underwent a major shift of emphasis, which led the public and private sectors to join forces to develop an open, diversified and innovative economy capable of bringing the country level with the other great international economic powers. The strategy recognized that the huge revenue from oil sales would come to an end in the near future and that until then this money would be reinvested in ambitious projects able to stimulate the Gulf states' economies into new directions and away from their dependence on oil and gas reserves. In the space of just a few years and at an incredible rate, the inhabitants of the UAE rebuilt their old economy based on pearl fishing and the slave trade to transform themselves into shrewd financiers and stockbrokers. What was once known as the Pirate Coast, due to raids on shipping in the Persian Gulf, thus rapidly became a center of international finance.

The country is currently home to around 50 banks (over half of which are foreign), flanked by various financial and investment consulting firms, numerous exchange offices, and large multinationals, such as Microsoft, IBM, Oracle, and CNN, attracted by the opportunity to conduct business freely and benefit from tax incentives. This economic policy has triggered property growth in the service sector comparable to that of the great Chinese cities, with an unprecedented building boom in the emirates of Abu Dhabi and Dubai. Financial centers are currently being completed in both cities, whose glittering futuristic buildings are becoming authentic symbols of modernity and dynamism. The towers designed by Carlos Ott for the National Bank of Dubai and that of Abu Dhabi have been followed by many other buildings, and countless more are planned for the coming years.

Dubai is rapidly establishing itself as the most important city for trade and services in the Gulf region, with ambitions to become an important international commercial hub in the near future. The city's International Financial Centre has been built from scratch with the consultation of Gensler Associates. This monumental complex covers an area of almost 500 acres (202 hectares), housing the premises of financial and service institutions which are arranged around The Gate, a massive arch-shaped building that symbolizes the city's economic solidity and ambition. This image is reinforced by the DIFC's elegant Emirates Towers, built on Sheikh Zayed Road, in an area that was until recently a stretch of inhospitable desert.

Abu Dhabi, on the other hand, has concentrated its symbols of economic power on the Corniche, running along the seafront behind the old town. Here imposing glass skyscrapers, such as the ADIA (Abu Dhabi Investment Authority) headquarters, alternate with elegant hotels like the Hilton Baynunah, creating the ideal setting to define an open, safe, and financially stable environment, where the leading local banks offer attractive packages for investors all over the world.

These cities already boast unique structures in both formal and technological terms, and other "wonders" will be inaugurated soon. The phenomenon is accompanied by the "Manhattanization" of the most important cities, whose skylines have suddenly acquired a plethora of soaring towers. Verticality, height, and slimness seem to be the most recurrent architectural themes in commercial buildings. These features have been selected as the most fitting to convey the idea of economic power, corporate prestige, and cultural identity of a country that has perhaps entered the process of globalization rather too quickly and without asking too many questions.

Architecture has thus become the most expressive means for displaying the nation's economic power to the world. The towers in question, with massive steel frames and gleaming polychrome glass skins, are equipped with the most sophisticated technological systems, whose efficiency and functionality have earned them the epithet "intelligent buildings." Sometimes they take the form of schizophrenic contortions that seek anti-structural forms for the sole pleasure of astounding, as though challenging the static and constructional values of architecture. The question of environmental sustainability has prompted the quest for new alternative energy sources and the construction of buildings with reduced energy consumption, able to function in a world without oil.

The architecture of these structures is highly varied, in some cases causing bewilderment by appearing as expressions of aesthetic exhibitionism with little architectural merit, in others capable of creating a bond (sometimes merely symbolic or narrative) with local tradition and history. These conceptual references are linked to traditional activities connected with the sea, the pure regular geometry of the triangle or the pyramid, and the calligraphic abstract motifs and arabesques of Islamic culture. However, sometimes they draw on Western archetypes that are alien to the country, such as the The Gate in Dubai, which emulates the great triumphant arches of Western architectural tradition; or the ADIA headquarters and the Strata Tower in Abu Dhabi, whose sinuous abstract forms are based on dynamic movement that seeks to integrate the setting with light and air. In many cases the buildings are self-referring, engaging with themselves alone and ignoring their surroundings, or feature forms justified by purely technological requirements, such as the Abu Dhabi World Trade Center at Al Raha Beach, designed by Foster + Partners. O.E.B.

National Bank of Dubai Building

DUBAI

NORR GROUP CONSULTANTS INT. LTD.
CARLOS OTT ARCHITECT

The headquarters building of the National Bank of Dubai is the result of an international competition held in the mid-1990s and won by Uruguayan architect Carlos Ott and NORR Group Consultants. Upon its completion in 1997, it was one of the first modern buildings in the city designed by internationally renowned architects, and – together with the nearby Etisalat Telecommunications Tower – it soon became a benchmark for the construction of the many high-rise buildings subsequently erected in Dubai.

The National Bank of Dubai stands on Baniyas Road, near the Sheraton Dubai Creek Hotel in Deira, the city's old downtown. It is a tall tower with a simple, austere form, which rapidly became an important landmark of modern Dubai, with its gleaming skyscrapers and luxurious hotels, and an icon on the downtown skyline.

The National Bank of Dubai has a singular yet simple form, characterized by two massive square-based pillars clad with granite, which rise either side of the structure and are visible from afar. They support the curved volume suspended above the atrium, further reinforcing the concept of the sail. The 407-ft (124-m) high building's unusual curved glass façade is reflected in the Creek, evoking the wind-filled sails of the merchants' dhows that have sailed these waters for centuries, thus creating a symbolic link with the city's age-old trading role. This connection is also echoed in the base housing the lobby, which is clad with panels of the same color as the waters of the Creek, while the stylized form of the aluminum roof is derived from the hull of a dhow. The bulging façade (locals refer affectionately to the building as the "Pregnant Lady") not only reflects the colors of the sky and water during the day, it also glows silver and gold at sunset.

The building is entirely intended for offices and is not completely open to the public and only the base is accessible to clients during normal working hours. O.E.B.

66 The imposing spatial presence of the bank is energized by its curved surface that reflects sunlight and the undulating waters of the Persian Gulf, creating an architecture that constantly changes its abstract appearance with especially evocative effects at dawn and sunset.

67 The main façade has a ship's keel profile which becomes more dynamic thanks to the linear aspect of the two supporting pillars at either end and contrasting textures in surface finish materials.

National Bank of Abu Dhabi Headquarters

ABU DHABI

Uruguayan architect Carlos Ott and his colleague Adel Almojil were the winners of the international competition held in 1995 for the design of the new headquarters of the National Bank of Abu Dhabi. The building was the first of a series of important commissions that the Montevideo-based firm received from the wealthy sheikhs of the UAE, who had the chance to note the dependability and expertise of the South American practice during its construction between 1996 and 1998.

The design of the building came just a few years after Ott's firm had won the prestigious competition for the Opéra Bastille in Paris, placing his name among the great stars of international architecture. It marked the beginning of the Middle East's enthusiastic embrace of prestigious global firms for the design of the new financial infrastructure required to handle the region's enormous wealth. The bank, whose construction took around three years, was completed in 2000 and required an investment of around 110 million U.S. dollars.

The 33-story tower was built to house the financial and commercial departments of the National Bank of Abu Dhabi. It therefore needed to be both functional and representative of the emirate's economic power. Its profile consists of a series of intersecting geometric shapes and features a double structure visible in the two volumes that compose it. Both of these have a pyramidal cross section and are rotated so that the two tips are positioned like mirror images. A third volume, smaller than those of the towers and clad with dark stone slabs, echoes the pyramid theme. It is positioned above the large entrance lobby, with its tip resting on the ground, and channels visitors towards the imposing entrance.

Greater figurative and compositional impact has been given to the entrance area by raising it on several steps and protecting it with an overhanging roof, while the entire part of the volume that defines this section of the building is separated from the rest of the tower by an empty space between the floors. On the other side a slender column supports and intersects the upturned pyramid, emphasizing the main entrance to the prestigious bank. A quadruple-height atrium provides access to the interior of the building and is lit by large transparent windows along the street front, offering interesting views into and out of the structure.

The building has a total floor area of around 375,000 sq ft (35,000 sq m), making it slightly smaller than the National Bank of Dubai. In accordance with the client's requests, the bank has a very simple, almost austere appearance. The characteristic skin of the building consists of sober gray glass, marked only by horizontal bands that project from the two main façades. O.E.B.

68 The tower may be seen as the sum of three distinct parts: its foundation; central body; and its crown. In fact, these elements have been created with different forms, materials, and colors to emphasize each one in its own way.

69 The façade of the atrium entrance is supported by a metallic tubular subframe with special steel couplings that bear the weight of large glass panels.

The Gate

DUBAI

The Gate is a modern reinterpretation of the triumphal arch, drawing parallels with other illustrious structures built all over the world in different periods: from the Arch of Augustus to the Arc de Triomphe, the Brandenburg Gate, and the Grande Arche de la Défense. It is the icon of Dubai's economic triumph and performs the symbolic function of a proud and enduring gateway to the city's dynamic district of fast-paced progress.

The building, designed by Gensler Associates, marks the entrance to the new Dubai International Financial Centre (DIFC) and is the focus of a more ambitious urban plan that features the construction of more important buildings, including the Emirates Towers, Park Towers, and the Liberty House, on a 457-acre (185-hectare) plot. The master plan, drawn up by the same London-based firm, coordinates the construction of a new hub destined to provide all the financial services necessary to make Dubai a hub of the global economy. Situated midway between the European and Asian stock exchanges, the DIFC aims to become an international financial center, comparable to New York, London, and Hong Kong. Consequently, The Gate is already an important symbol for the entire city.

Its strategic position in relation to the city center and the international airport valorizes the area that will house the headquarters of the UAE's leading economic and financial institutions, including the Central Bank and the Stock Exchange. The master plan for the district features the strict zoning of the various activities, with six sectors connected and integrated by innovative IT services. The result is an autonomous urban complex in the elegant central avenue, which intentionally evokes the Champs-Elysées in Paris. Its most distinctive landmark is The Gate – the monumental entrance to the city of progress and development.

However, the DIFC does not consist merely of offices, but features a functional mixture of residential units, cultural venues, hotels, shopping malls, and everything else expected of a cosmopolitan city that offers a luxurious, multicultural, hi-tech lifestyle. An automated transport system with moving walkways connects the various sectors of the Financial Centre.

70 Signalling the presence of a central arterial road reminiscent of the Parisian Champs-Elysée, the Gate rises up in the heart of the same area as the Dubai International Financial Centre. This modern structure is one of the few office buildings that is not a skyscraper.

71 Including a lake, the Gate is part of a fully landscaped green space surrounded by other dazzling structures that accommodate service sector businesses connected to the world of finance and economics.

71

The actual structure of The Gate is formed by two solid pillar-like towers, 15 stories tall, topped by a massive architrave embellished with a steel grid. The outermost masonry façades are clad with light-colored stone slabs arranged in horizontal bands, while the remaining ones have large glass curtain walls. These materials give the building a powerful, austere appearance, quite unlike that of any other structure in the area. The most prestigious offices are located behind the unbroken glass band of the architrave, above and below which slit-like windows are arranged in a vaguely Arabian-style decorative pattern. The building rises from a pool in a public plaza. The water not only cools the air temperature, but also guides visitors wishing to enter the DIFC through the gateway. O.E.B.

72-73 The Gate is located on an axis with the World Trade Center and the Emirates Twin Towers, which establishes a strong formal urban relationship with other iconic components of the city that as a whole are "Manhattanizing" the financial district.

73 The Gate interiors are designed with maximum sophistication and elegance. Reflective materials were selected to intensify the play of light while expensive flooring and fine furnishings all testify to the economic power and financial strength of the institutions that it accommodates.

74 A circular lake contributes to the design of this open space. When the interior of the ground floor is illuminated, light reflects on the water, creating a magical play of mirrored and refracted light.

75 Stone slabs designed with decorative motifs recalling the friezes on the Arc de Triomphe in Paris form a part of the external enclosure. A curtain wall finishes the covered walkway in a different style.

Abu Dhabi Investment Authority Tower

ABU DHABI

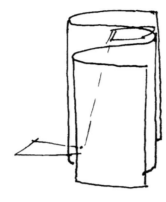

Completed in 2006, the ADIA headquarters is undoubtedly one of the most elegant and alluring skyscrapers in Abu Dhabi. Its name is derived from the initials of the client that commissioned it: the Abu Dhabi Investment Authority, one of the most important government investment companies. The international architecture practice of Kohn Pedersen Fox Associates was entrusted with the task of designing a unique, sophisticated building that reinterpreted some of the features of the local architectural tradition with a modern twist. Situated where the buildings of the historic district meet the street grid of the modern city, the ADIA Tower is an important landmark for both the inhabitants of Abu Dhabi and shipping in the Persian Gulf.

In order to satisfy the client's requests, the architects designed a tower that symbolically revives the themes of the hanging garden and the inner courtyard of traditional Arabian houses. These features are present in the public areas of the building and the meeting rooms housed on each of its 35 floors.

76 top The silhouette of the Abu Dhabi Investment Authority Tower is inspired by the soft and undulating line of a crumpled piece of paper around three central supports. This formal design endows the structure with a characteristic dynamism that distinguishes it from all other buildings.

76 bottom This typical blueprint shows the space distribution with the central common core that contains the vertical connections, utilities unit, and overlooks the atrium from full height, as well as the two lateral blocks that accommodate office space.

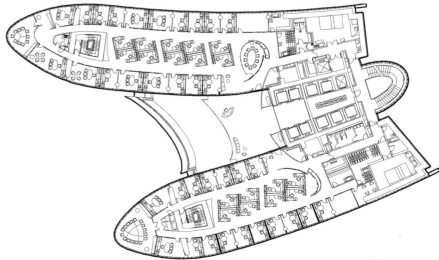

76-77 This skyscraper is one of the buildings that best characterize the architectural look of the capital's waterfront, whether because of its morphology or conformity to transparent and lightweight surface finish materials. It is especially visible to those on the waters around the city.

77 bottom The organization of this floor plan results from the trapezoidal shape of the building's lot, and is completed by generous, open, and sloping spaces that separate the building from the public thoroughfares.

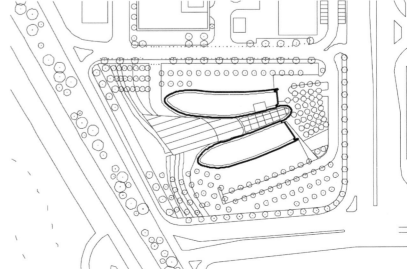

Here lush vegetation evokes the concept of the hanging garden, almost as though it were the extension of the luxuriant greenery outside the building.

The gardens also overlook the soaring central atrium, which rises throughout the entire height of the building, reinterpreting the concept of the inner courtyard of traditional Islamic architecture. The tower is characterized by its tall slender silhouette, the lightness of its volumes, the rhythmic cleanliness of its façades, and its transparency.

The most significant element of the building is undoubtedly the continuous line that generates the two curved wings, like a sheet of corrugated card. These structures occupy a trapezoidal-shaped site whose form is determined by the distortion of the urban grid at that point. While the curved north-facing wing housing the offices is aligned with the orthogonal street plan, the south-facing wing is slightly rotated to open towards the sea and face Mecca. The space between the two structures houses the vertical atrium, which occupies the entire height of the building and contains the elevator shafts, stairwells, and service areas. It is projected beyond the tower by a steel pergola that marks the entrance to the building. The functional design of the tower built to house the bank's services and executive functions is completed by a 250-seat auditorium near the atrium. In order to ensure the comfort of its occupants, the tall atrium acts as a solar chimney, offering natural ventilation to dissipate the heat that accumulates inside the building and thus helping to cool the workspaces. Special screens have been used to protect the areas of the atrium subject to greatest amount of sunlight at the hottest times of day.

The distinctive profile of the ADIA Tower is derived from the image of a book opening towards the infinite ocean in a welcoming gesture. Nonetheless, the disjointed volumes of the wings, the concept of a spiral enveloping the façades, and the dematerializing effect of the top of the building create a variable and even unstable form of architecture, capable of assuming a dynamic character.   O.E.B.

78 The lower part of this skyscraper was designed according to a soft and continuous line that wraps back on itself in such a way as to create a structure that defines a kind of rhythmic yet formal dynamic.

79 The Abu Dhabi Investment Authority Tower, facing the waters of the Persian Gulf, looks onto an elegant green space along the Abu Dhabi Corniche quarter, not far from the Baynunah Hilton Hotel.

80 top This building's entrance is highlighted by a type of "pronaos" or vestibule in steel sections, supported by a forest of tapered columns that are not perpendicular to the floor in order to limit any tectonic movement.

80 bottom The reception area is the only public access point to the building, and it is possible to monitor from here, round the clock, everyone who enters the building. This is vital for ensuring the required standard of security for a commercial structure.

80-81 The soft lines that define this structure were incorporated into the design of the vertical connections. The large curvilinear staircase was conceived as a type of "architectural promenade" that allows people to enjoy a view of the capital's development.

Abu Dhabi Investment
Authority Tower

82 and 83 The entrance is
defined by a large atrium, the
height of the building, facing
onto the common areas on
various levels. This formal design
and serves to guarantee a more
comfortable interior temperature.
Elegant interior surface finishes
have maximum functionality.
Rich marbles were utilized

Al Jaber Tower

Dubai Media City

Media One Tower

DUBAI

Dubai Media City will be the new urban hub dedicated to media organizations situated at the crossroads between the economies of Asia, Europe, and Africa. The idea for the project was conceived by Sheikh Mohammed bin Rashid Al Maktoum, Prime Minister and Vice President of the United Arab Emirates, who believed that the country's economic and social development should also encompass technological innovation, information, research, and knowledge, as befitting a modern economy. The Media One Tower in Dubai was thus designed as the ideal place to conduct business and commerce in the spheres of media, communications and marketing, publishing, music, film and entertainment, broadcasting, and information. This tower offers everything required for investors in the sector, in an open flexible environment with support structures, where capital can circulate freely and income is not subject to taxation.

The Media One Tower will be located at the entrance to Dubai Media City, opposite Dubai Marina and overlooking the artificial Palm Jumeirah island. Also known as the Al Jaber Tower, the 41-story structure will be a distinctive feature on the Dubai skyline. It will not only house the headquarters of leading companies, but also a conference center equipped with state-of-the art technologies and a hotel occupying the first 20 floors, with 270 luxurious rooms, gyms, a swimming pool, stores, and restaurants. The offices will be housed on the upper floors, between the 21st and 40th floors, and will be occupied mainly by companies operating in the field of digital communications.

The building will consist of a completely glazed 558-ft (170-m) tall tower with a flatiron-shaped plan and a seven-floor podium with a curved plan.

This reinforced concrete plinth with a metal exoskeleton will have the dual function of screening and protecting the parking lot that it houses. The complex will be characterized by a sort of stone-clad arch applied to the façade, which will rise to the fifth floor to mark the building's main entrance.

84 This 558-ft (170-m) tower is completely covered with windows and characterized by a geometric design resulting from the metal framework of the special glass, while the foundation consists of a reinforced concrete footing covered with modular steel panels.

85 The main entrance expands from the base of the tower and incorporates a monumental portal bearing the name of the building that intersects with the height of the fifth floor.

DEWAN ARCHITECTS & ENGINEERS · JUNG BRANNEN ASSOCIATES

The structure will have a total floor area of around 807,000 sq ft (75,000 sq m).

The design for the glass skin is marked by a regular metal grid, which will create an almost kinetic effect due to the formal characteristics of the building. It boasts unique features and is designed to modulate both the reflection and refraction of light and the views from within the building. The tower will have several separate entrances and the different functions housed on the various levels are served by elevators, the fastest of which will travel at 16.4 ft (5 m) per second (11.2 miles per hour/18 km/h). A ground-floor entrance, dedicated exclusively to the offices, is connected to the reception area of the hotel, while a large parking lot will be housed on the basement floor and the seven floors above it to ensure sufficient parking space for the hotel guests. High-speed wireless Internet connections and cutting-edge equipment will be available throughout the building, which has been designed for upwardly mobile entrepreneurs and dynamic businesspeople.

Many different firms participated in the design of the tower, including Dewan Architects and Engineers and Jung Brannen Associates for the architectural design, BG&E for the structural engineering, Badri and Bensouda for the landscaping, LWDesign for the interiors, DPA for the lighting, and Hepher Project Management as project manager. O.E.B.

Media one Tower

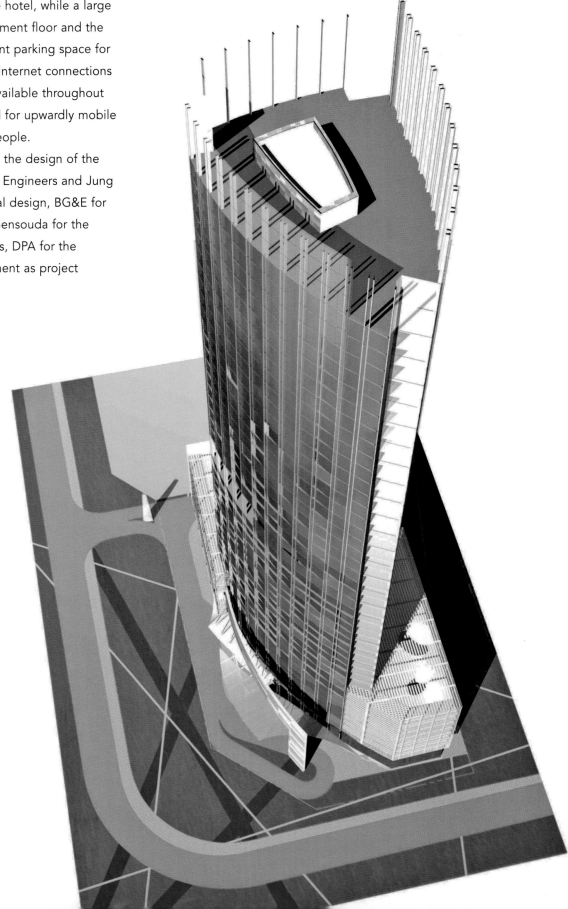

86 3D graphic representations make it possible to appreciate the tower's construction, including the architectural proportions of its diverse parts and the characteristic design of its steam iron-shaped form.

87 The elegant silhouette of this skyscraper has an exterior that seems to vibrate chromatically when light shines on it during different hours of the day. Revealing its function, the tower has a large, ground-level multimedia screen broadcasting uninterrupted advertising images.

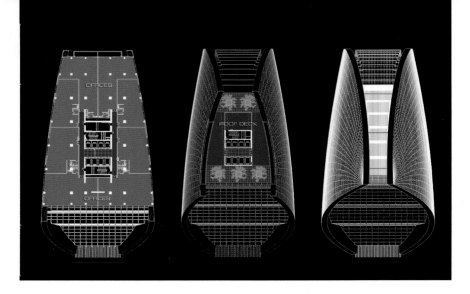

Sheth Tower Iris Bay

DUBAI

Situated in the nerve center of Dubai, next to the Burj Khalifa on Sheikh Zayed Road, the Iris Bay has been designed by WS Atkins & Partners, one of the four largest architecture and engineering firms in the world. It is a demonstration of how, in the city of Arabian excess, a building can be distinctive and imposing without having to be super-tall.

Characterized by a revolutionary half-moon form and divided into 32 floors cantilevered on huge concrete pillars, the tower will stand 558 ft (170 m) tall. It will appear suspended above a four-story podium with a double-height arcade housing retail spaces, while the upper floors will house offices (ranging from 1,109 to 4,843 sq ft/103 to 450 sq m), with a total floor area of over 880,000 sq ft (82,000 sq m).

The building is arranged so that its main façade will overlook Sheikh Zayed Road, the city's principal thoroughfare, and will consist of two identical curved shells housing the transparent glass façades. The completely glazed main façade will be formed of rotated panels set at seven different angles in order to create a faceted effect that changes according to the light reflected off the glass at different times of day. The rear façade will be narrower and less open, appearing as a continuous curve dotted with regularly spaced balconies at different levels, while the other façades will be more closed. Public areas, including prayer rooms, a gym and an outdoor

swimming pool, will be housed in the band between the podium of the building and the tower above.

The originality of the project lies in the fact that it tackles problems of sustainability by seeking energy-saving design systems that adapt several principles of traditional Arabian architecture developed to ensure environmental comfort. A natural ventilation system will cool the building, whose façades have been designed to aid the circulation of the cool night air through strategically arranged perforations.

88 and 89 This architecture is based upon principles of environmental sustainability, where the latest cooling system research has influenced design choices. A naturally assisted ventilation system allows fresh air to circulate inside the building, decreasing interior temperature. Air entering the lower part of the tower is cooled when it comes into contact with water in basement reservoirs as well as the waterfall, that defines the unique entrance on Sheikh Zayad Road. Amorphous silicon photovoltaic panels integrated into the main façade produce a reasonable quantity of electricity in addition to acting as blinds.

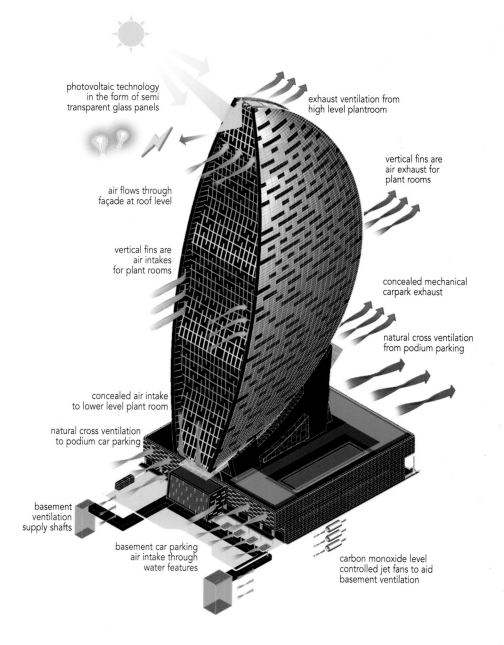

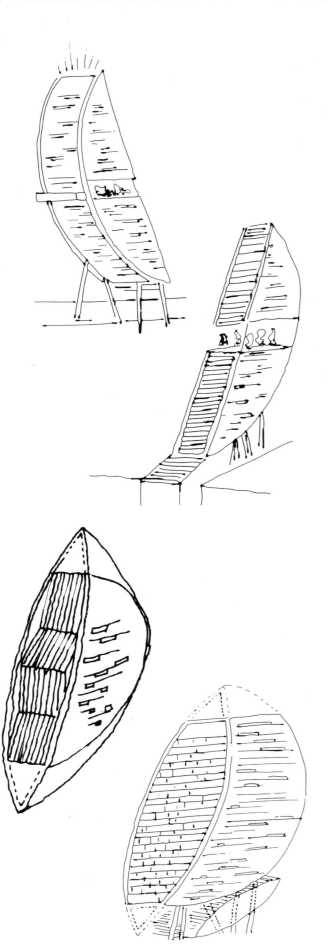

There will be an air vent at ground level on the side overlooking Sheikh Zayed Road, through which air will enter the building and be cooled by a water wall. The cool air will then be conveyed to the upper floors, lowering the temperature of the interiors, before leaving the building through the roof. This natural cooling system will be supplemented by an artificial one necessary to control the levels of carbon monoxide in the underground parking lot, which will have 920 spaces on three levels.

The maintenance and service rooms will be situated halfway up the tower to maximize the efficiency of distribution of the technical systems. A mesh of transparent photovoltaic panels will be built into the glazing of the main façade and will act as a brise-soleil, while the windows on the building's short sides are reduced to narrow slits in the opaque skin, in order to minimize solar heat gain. The podium and the top of the tower will feature roof gardens, which will enhance the sense of wellbeing of the building's occupants.   O.E.B.

90 left These study sketches demonstrate a desire to research formal solutions and spatial innovations capable of giving iconic impact to the design.

90 right Iris Bay will become especially fascinating at night, when artificial light illuminating its interiors will filter through the mosaic of apertures that mark its lateral facings with different shapes. The diverse angles of

the glass windows making up the main façade evoke the image of the sea rippling with waves.

91 The secondary façade is turned towards the waterfront at Business Bay. The four lower levels have equivalent façades to the one looking onto Sheikh Zayad Road, while the upper part of the building consists of the convex, half-moon shaped façade.

0-14

DUBAI

The as yet unbuilt O-14 office tower, designed by New York architects Reiser and Umemoto, will be a glittering icon of cosmopolitan life, where commerce and culture merge in a unique architectural structure in the heart of Dubai's Business Bay, making it the emblem of an ambitious project to transform the UAE into a nerve center for global business and commerce. This enormous area is arranged like a city within the city, forming an extension of Dubai Creek from Ras al Khor to Sheikh Zayed Road.

The 22-story commercial tower known as 0-14 will have a total floor area of approximately 150,000 sq ft (14,000 sq m), plus four underground levels housing a 416-space parking lot. The ground floor and mezzanine are home to a spacious lobby and several stores, while the two floors immediately above form a sort of indoor plaza with a showroom, semi-public areas, and a restaurant with a large terrace overlooking the Creek. An entire floor at the top of the tower will house the necessary service machinery.

The distinctive design feature of the building is its skin, which will take the form of a 16-inch (40-cm) thick concrete shell, subverting the traditional rules of modern architecture by becoming the structural frame of the entire building, in conjunction with the central elevator core. This design

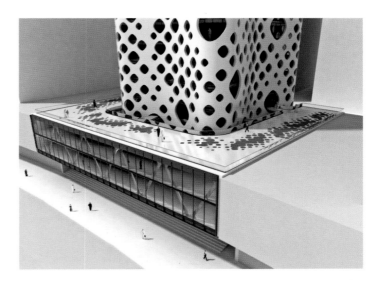

92-93 The 15.75-inch (40-cm) thick envelope was created as a concrete structural shell, which porosity studies have shown will regulate interior levels of illumination and ventilation.

93 The large terrace positioned above the lower level offers privileged views of the surrounding cityscape, and incorporates protected green areas and spaces for relaxation.

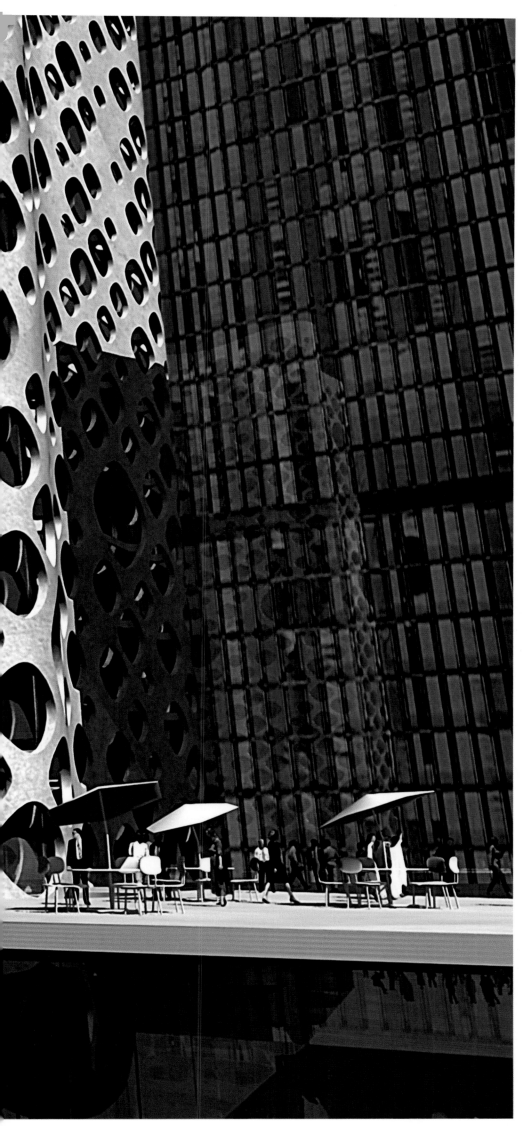

ensures the maximum flexibility of the interiors, unhindered by columns or other structural elements. It will also allow considerable energy savings, as a space of about 40 inches (101 cm) will separate the concrete shell from the inner glass skin, and so form a ventilated façade that will create a passive cooling system by means of the stack effect.

Structural and energy functions aside, the tower's skin will be a spectacular sight, with a pattern reminiscent of lace or snakeskin. It will consist of a rigid membrane perforated by over 1,000 rhomboidal holes of various sizes that will maximize its permeability, allowing the natural lighting of the interiors and offering the building's occupants stunning views over the city. The distribution of the holes has been calculated on the basis of structural criteria, but also according to the need for different levels of light and sun exposure in the various parts of the building. The pattern of the shell will be further emphasized by the building's irregular shape, which rises from a butterfly-shaped plan to form a sinuous volume that will become a distinctive landmark of this "Oriental Manhattan."

In keeping with the spirit of innovation and flexibility required by a building of this type, the areas destined for offices can be laid out as wished, for the floor plan is almost completely flexible, with the exception of the central core (which will house the five elevators and a double flight of stairs) and the service block. Consequently, clients can choose from different sized offices, with two, three or four units on each floor. In special circumstances it will be possible to create private links between levels in order increase the total floor area. O.E.B.

94-95 In the shade of the great porous tower, the wide terrace overlooking Business Bay accommodates customers in this restaurant that enjoys a panoramic view of the city from the third floor.

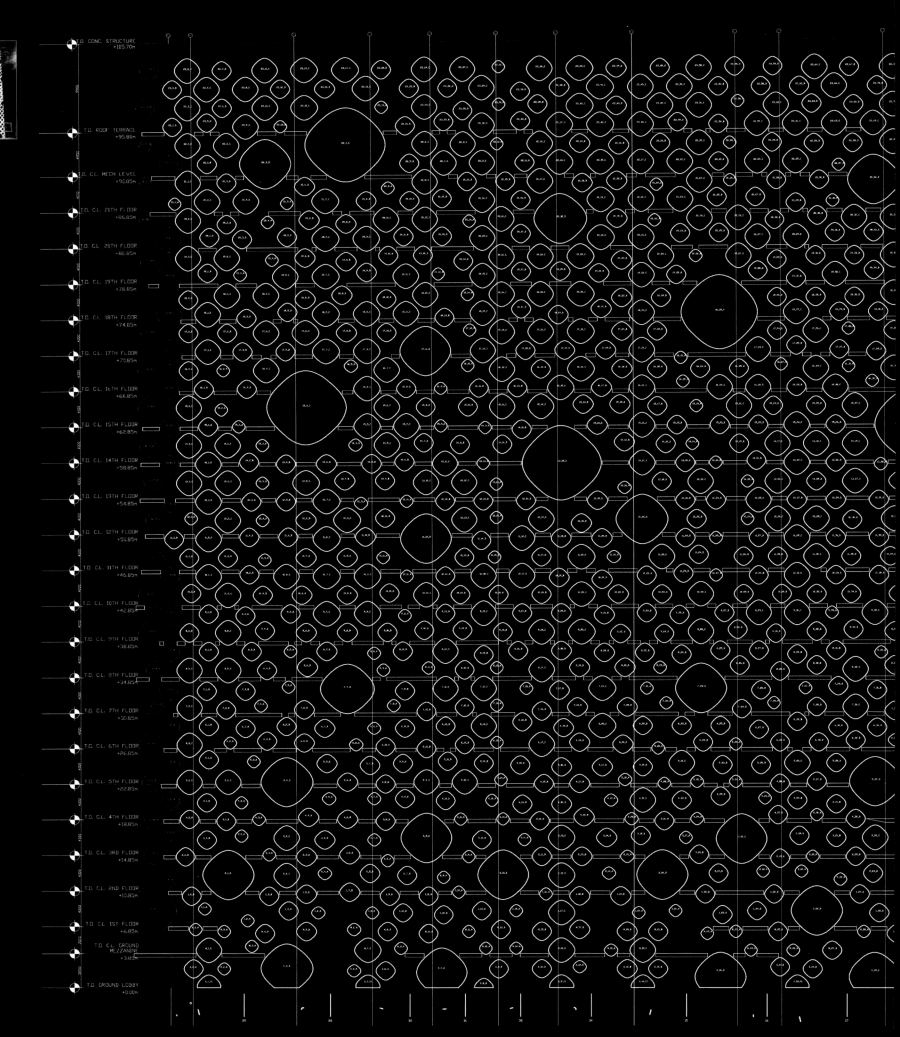

T.O. CONC. STRUCTURE
+105.70m

T.O. ROOF TERRACE
+95.80m

T.O. C.L. MECH LEVEL
+90.85m

T.O. C.L. 21TH FLOOR
+86.85m

T.O. C.L. 20TH FLOOR
+82.85m

T.O. C.L. 19TH FLOOR
+78.85m

T.O. C.L. 18TH FLOOR
+74.85m

T.O. C.L. 17TH FLOOR
+70.85m

T.O. C.L. 16TH FLOOR
+66.85m

T.O. C.L. 15TH FLOOR
+62.85m

T.O. C.L. 14TH FLOOR
+58.85m

T.O. C.L. 13TH FLOOR
+54.85m

T.O. C.L. 12TH FLOOR
+50.85m

T.O. C.L. 11TH FLOOR
+46.85m

T.O. C.L. 10TH FLOOR
+42.85m

T.O. C.L. 9TH FLOOR
+38.85m

T.O. C.L. 8TH FLOOR
+34.85m

T.O. C.L. 7TH FLOOR
+30.85m

T.O. C.L. 6TH FLOOR
+26.85m

T.O. C.L. 5TH FLOOR
+22.85m

T.O. C.L. 4TH FLOOR
+18.85m

T.O. C.L. 3RD FLOOR
+14.85m

T.O. C.L. 2ND FLOOR
+10.85m

T.O. C.L. 1ST FLOOR
+6.85m

T.O. C.L. GROUND
MEZZANINE
+3.85m

T.O. GROUND LOBBY
+0.00m

O-14

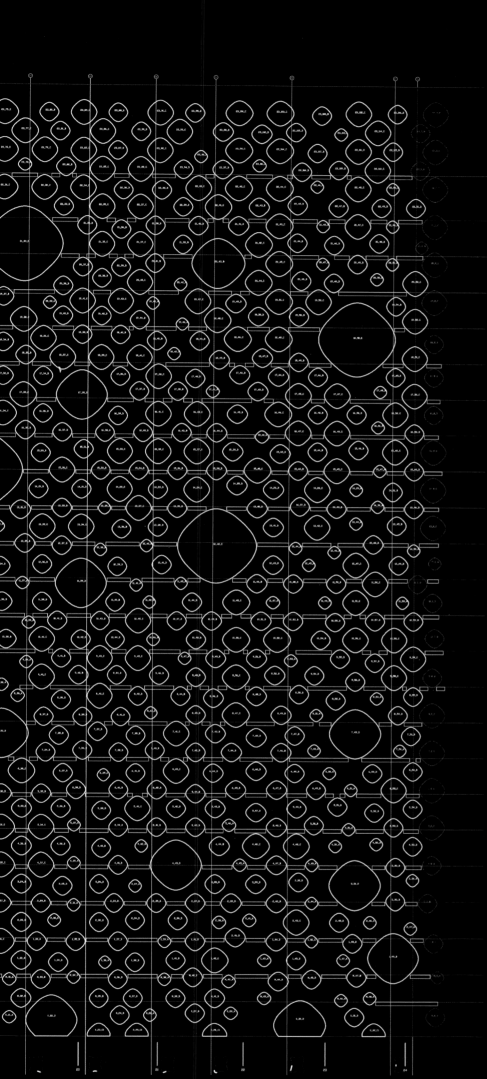

96-97 The very original lace-inspired tower enclosure is pierced with more than 1,000 rhomboidal openings of different sizes. Their placement is not random but is based on a very precise study that examined structural aspects, taking into account the need to maximize light permeability and the desire to frame the most evocative panoramic views.

97 This construction solution creates an original scenic effect that is especially evident in the evening and at night when artificial light filters from inside the building.

98-99 Created with glass panes throughout, these walls were moved back by about 3.3 ft (1 m) from the exterior concrete enclosure to create an airy façade that is able to generate a passive cooling system through a chimney effect.

98 bottom The highest level of the tower accommodates rooms that house the technical systems necessary for the tower's function. The remaining roof area is devoted to a pass-through terrace punctuated by flowerpots whose forms are reminiscent of the shapes in the enclosure's cutouts.

99 bottom A three-level basement houses the common areas, the showroom, the bars, and restaurant, connecting to the rest of the tower via glass tunnels that link through rhomboidal openings in the structural shell.

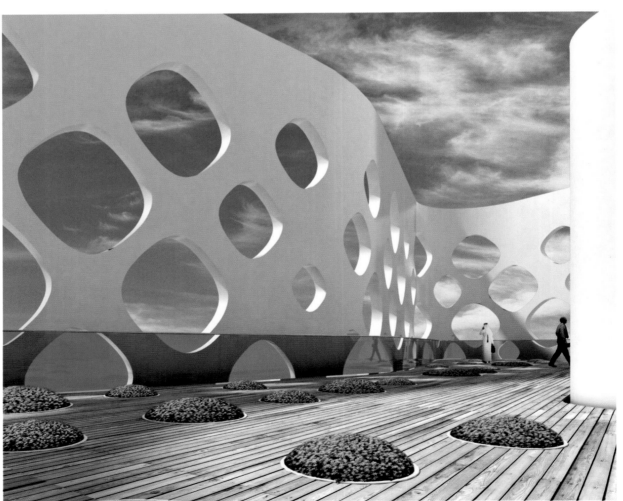

norr group, hazel w.s. wong *(em*
& merrill llp *(burj khalifa)* - foster
owings & merrill llp *(sun tower)* - o
associates *(signature towers)* - llewe
yeang sdn. bhd. *(eco bay)* - sy
associates *(the opus)*

mixed use

ates twin towers) - skidmore, owings

+ partners *(the index)* - skidmore,

ha *(dubai renaissance)* - zaha hadid &

n davies yeang, t.r. hamzah &

arite *(khaledya)* - zaha hadid &

mixed use

Mixed-use complexes constitute an excellent property investment due to the different functions that they encompass. They generally combine offices and residential units, sometimes with the addition of a hotel. This mixture allows the shared use of certain technological and functional facilities, such as lobbies, spas, and commercial areas. The plan of such complexes generally follows one of two typical layouts. In the first of these, the various functions are housed in separate structures built on a shared podium, where maintenance and service rooms and parking spaces are located on the basement floors, with entrance and retail areas above. The large air-conditioned podium houses the usual urban public spaces that do not exist outdoors in the Gulf area, due to the excessively high temperatures. Shops, boutiques, and department stores are arranged on several levels around huge entrance halls. The second type of layout is represented by a single multipurpose building housing the various activities and is exemplified by the skyscraper, whose façades allow floors with residential units to be combined with others housing office space. Indeed, while the internal layout of commercial areas in such a building tends to favor solutions aimed at reducing structural obstacles – both in the plan and on the façades – in order to allow maximum flexibility, the new residential skyscrapers also strive to maximize openness. The curtain wall – from the simplest to the most sophisticated versions, such as the Al Sharq Tower designed by Skidmore, Owings and Merrill LLP (SOM) – is admirably suited to both functions.

In terms of environmental sustainability, aimed particularly at achieving energy savings for the air-conditioning of the structure, massive façades exploiting the thermal inertia of the materials have given way to high-performance double skins, which often feature external shading systems to protect the building from solar radiation (e.g. the designs by Foster + Partners). A tower also allows each of the functions to be located at the ideal height, with residential units and hotels on the upper floors to enjoy the best views, and commercial areas on the more easily accessible lower levels. In this respect the buildings can become huge complex structures, where the theme of accessibility and separation of the internal circulation routes leads to the development of innovative and interesting designs.

The 2005/06 competition for the development of Dubai's central Business Bay district played an important role in the city's architectural debate, not only because it marked the definitive involvement of international "starchitects" in the expansion of this part of the Middle East, which has become a laboratory for experiments in modern architecture, but also due to the innovative solutions developed for mixed-use towers. The contest was won by Zaha Hadid, who interpreted functional complexity with a specific formal configuration based on the torsion and intersection of three towers to allow the sharing of public spaces and also on the separation of circulation routes within the buildings. However, Reiser and Umemoto also proposed a technical invention with evocative forms and Rem Koolhaas (OMA) used the opportunity for proposing the design of a megastructure. Indeed, Koolhaas' Dubai Renaissance is an experiment in which the traditional skyscraper building type is succeeded by an enormous blade-shaped structure that forms a vertical city, organized according to a vertical zoning plan, alternated with large public spaces that occupy entire double-story levels. However, while the hierarchical division of the circulation routes in Koolhaas's competition entry is somewhat cumbersome, those featured in Norman Foster's elegant solution for The Index, another example of a mixed-use tower, are stunningly rational.

This extraordinary expansion of the property market in this region has allowed the big names in international architecture to indulge their creativity, particularly when expressed in state-of-the-art projects featuring cutting-edge formal, structural, and technological devices. Competition among the various developers is primarily based on the iconic value or distinctive image of the building, which gives the investment the necessary prestige and exclusiveness to distinguish it from its neighbors and emerge as a landmark on the urban panorama. This competition was initially fueled by the developers' own unknown technical studios, which designed buildings drawing on the traditional Islamic decorative repertoire and Arabian mythology (with mixed results). However, the arrival in the region of the leading names in contemporary architecture, dominated by the power of the image, has given rise to a clash of cultures that risks creating self-referring structures, forming an urban landscape characterized by a sort of visual pollution. An interesting new approach is offered by OMA's efforts to adopt strikingly simple pure abstract shapes, whose formal results are even more efficient and monumental in terms of impact on the urban fabric.   L.D.

Emirates Twin Towers

DUBAI

The Emirates Towers in Dubai, completed in April 2000, have become a landmark that testifies to the state's rapid development, which it has been relentlessly pursuing for over a decade. Designed by Norr Group Consultants International with Hazel W.S. Wong, the twin towers stand out against the blue sky of Dubai, rising from Sheikh Zayed Road, one of the city's most important highways, to a height of 1,163 and 1,014 ft (354 and 309 m) respectively. The towers are part of a new urban expansion project and mark the boundary of the Dubai International Financial Centre (DIFC), contrasting with another of the city's icons – The Gate building.

At the time of their construction, the towers were among the 20 tallest buildings in the world and among the first skyscrapers to be built in the Middle East. They are an impressive example of the popular architectural design of using twin buildings, which has been used in many cities around the world, notably New York's Twin Towers, Chicago's Marina City, and more recently the Petronas Towers in Kuala Lumpur.

The style of the Emirates Towers is an intentional blend of high-tech and craftmanship, innovation and tradition, and features the same approach to design that distinguishes much of the new architecture of the United Arab Emirates. Here simple elementary forms derived from the local culture are combined with innovative materials and technology in an attempt to establish an ideal bond between past and future. In this case the connection with the past is made via the geometric forms of the triangle and the pyramid, which are two popular shapes in Arabian culture. They are constantly repeated in the plan of the two towers, the design of their roofs, their floor patterns, and in numerous other details.

The towers rise curvaceously from a stepped podium set in a park. Their silhouette is created from the intersection of two solids, a cylinder and a triangular-based prism, whose formal nature has been intentionally emphasized by the use of different materials, colors, and transparency for the exterior. The skin of the towers is made from steel, copper and various shades of reflective glass, giving the building a highly distinctive appearance that changes with the light. It is particularly spectacular at night thanks to a carefully designed lighting system that illuminates the various sections of the two towers.

104 The Dubai International Financial Centre intersects with an important central axis where the Gate Building also stands, lining up with other significant buildings in the city, such as the World Trade Center and the Emirates Towers.

105 Geometric forms recall abstract drawings where recurrent symbolic motifs of the triangle, rectangle, and pyramid stand out against the background of the clear Dubai sky in plays of shadow and reflection.

Emirates Twin Towers

The base not only gives the towers a monumental appearance, but also serves to link them. It houses stores, restaurants, covered parking for 1,800 cars, and a spectacular lobby, embellished with waterfalls and precious marble. Granite has been used to clad the base, emphasizing its functional link with the ground and contrasting it with the adjacent highways.

The highest tower is known as the Emirates Office Tower and houses offices, conference rooms, and a business

center, while the shorter one is called the Jumeirah Emirates Towers Hotel and has approximately 400 rooms on 48 floors. Its facilities include conference rooms, bars, restaurants, a ballroom, a fitness center, and swimming pools.

This tower has a full-height central lobby around which the different levels of the hotel are arranged and which houses the steel elevators that serve the luxurious suites with their fabulous views over the city. O.E.B.

106-107 The two towers, though adhering to the classic architectural design of twin buildings, differ in height. Until the dawn of the 21st century, they were among the 20 highest buildings in the world and among the first buildings in the Middle East to have reached dizzy heights.

108 One of the most recognizable elements in the Emirates Towers is the highest one. To put final emphasis on the narrowness and upward rise of this part of the building, NORR Consultants International erected a spire at the top of the pyramid-shaped roof.

109 top In a "double play," the two towers mirror each other on the reflective surfaces of their façades, creating a magical illusion.

109 bottom To highlight their upward rise to the sky, the towers take shape in two 3D geometric forms with triangular foundations, incorporating cylindrical elements that are completely covered in polished glass.

110-111 The lower tower's curved façade curtain wall envelops the interior space the full height of the building, with overlooking hotel room corridors and glass elevators from which it is possible to enjoy great views of the city.

112 Accommodating a luxury five-star hotel, the atrium occupies the full height of the tower. The atrium holds the bank of elevators leading to the various floors and hotel room corridors overlook open space. The hotel lobby is located on the ground floor.

113 top and bottom Luxury boutiques offer exclusive products for sale. The bar on the top floor offers extraordinary views over the city of Dubai.

113 center The atrium entrance to the office tower has a two-floor high ceiling and is embellished with fine surface finish materials. To show them off, overhead lighting shines through a glass ceiling. The hotel's interiors have been carefully thought out, down to the last detail, to ensure that guests feel surrounded by a unique and refined ambience.

NORR GROUP . HAZEL W.S . WONG

NORR GROUP, HAZEL W.S. WONG

114 Due to their envelope
of reflective aluminum, copper,
and glass panelling, the towers
change color according to the
viewer's perspective, reflecting the
desert sun during daylight hours.

115 Through repetition,
the entrance emphasizes the
geometric triangle motif in its
proportions, underlining the
monumentality of this building
with a cantilevered roof.

Burj Khalifa

DUBAI

The Burj Khalifa, formerly known as Burj Dubai, does not simply aim to be the world's tallest skyscraper, but also the symbol of the city's increasingly important global role, becoming the icon of a prosperous, dynamic, and successful Middle East capable of asserting itself internationally in both economic and cultural terms. The tower is the focus of the new Downtown Burj Khalifa development adjoining Sheikh Zayed Road, a 500-acre (200-hectare) area featuring high- and low-rise office, hotel, and apartment buildings; the Dubai Mall, one of the largest shopping areas in the world; and a large park with a 130,000-sq-ft (12,000-sq-m) artificial lake from which the Burj Khalifa itself emerges, reflected in the waters to create an even more stunning effect.

he competition to build the world's tallest building is still as fierce as ever, and for this reason the final height of the skyscraper – that has been inaugurated on 4 January 2010 – has long been kept secret: the actual height of the tower is 2,716.5 ft (828 m), with more than 160 floors. The plan features a total floor area of over 3 million sq ft (278,000 sq m), with the first 37 floors occupied by an Armani Hotel, the first of its kind, luxury apartments on the successive 64 floors, offices and suites above the 109th floor, and telecommunications equipment on the roof. The 123rd floor houses a lobby for residents with an indoor/outdoor observation deck above, while the 78th floor has an outdoor swimming pool. The imposing podium houses further sports facilities and restaurants.

The design, created by Skidmore, Owings and Merrill LLP (SOM) (the winner of the competition held by Emaar Properties PJSC, one of the leading property developers in the Middle East) solves the complex structural problems associated with a building of this size by using a triple-lobed footprint based on an abstract version of the common desert flower *Hymenocallis* and references to traditional local architecture, associated with a geometric grid that echoes the abstract decorations of Islamic art. The Y-shaped plan ensures the natural lighting of the interiors and maximizes views over the city. From a static point of view it allows the construction of a central core with a hexagonal base housing elevator shafts and stairwells, reinforced by

three wings that buttress each other against the horizontal force of the wind and seismic loads. Aerodynamic studies during the design stage led the building's engineers to rotate it through 120 degrees to reduce stress from prevailing winds. The building tapers upward and each lobe features step-backs arranged in a spiral pattern, resulting in the progressive transformation of the floor plan. This design also prevents the formation of wind vortexes.

The complexity of the project is reflected in its construction. The tower is made of reinforced concrete up to the 155th floor, while the upper part has a steel frame structure. It is built on foundations with piles buried over 164 ft (50 m) deep. The composition of the concrete was carefully controlled, not only because it needed to be pumped to an unprecedented height of over 1,740 ft (530 m) (establishing yet another world record), but also to ensure the necessary structural strength to withstand the city's extreme climate, with differences of up to 15°F between the base and the top of the tower. Accurate calculations of the variations in temperature, humidity (up to 30 percent less at the top of the building than at its base), and air density (up to 10 percent lower at the top) using satellite-gathered data, allowed the designers to utilize high-efficiency engineering solutions capable of reducing energy consumption. The cladding of the building consists of reflective glazing and aluminum and textured stainless steel spandrel panels with vertical tubular fins. Two of the world's fastest double-decker elevators serve the tower, allowing the dimensions of the elevator shafts and stairwells to be reduced without diminishing passenger capacity.   L.D.

116 Displayed during the presentation of the project, this photo depicts the architectural model of the skyscraper that dominates the new development area of Downtown Burj Khalifa.

117 The tower – 2,716.5 ft (828 m) high – is based on a Y-shaped design. The spaces in the three branches are graded in a spiral line that rises with the height of the structure.

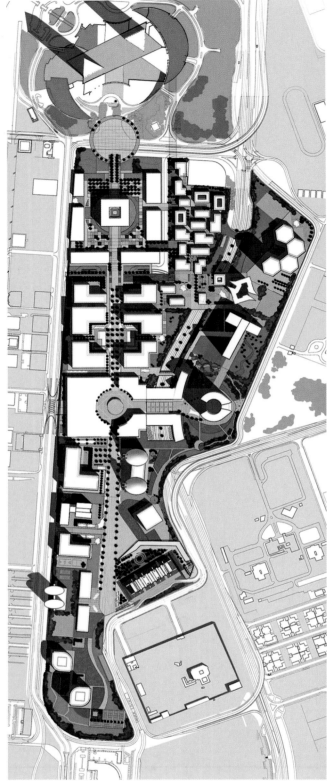

118 left In this three-dimensional illustration, you can distinctly see – starting from below – the block of offices, the three-level lobby, and the upper floors designated for apartments with prestigious penthouses at the top.

118 right This skyscraper is located on a lot along with the Dubai International Financial Centre, at the low right of the drawing, where you can see its main vertical axis, and the Emirates Towers above.

The Index

DUBAI

The Index, previously known as One Central Park, is a 1,076-ft (328-m) tall skyscraper with 80 floors currently under construction in the Dubai International Finance Centre, the new financial hub to the south of Sheikh Zayed Road. The unique feature of the project, designed by Foster + Partners in 2005, lies in the decision to highlight not only the building's structural reinforced concrete frame, but also the functional organization of its elevation. The vertical structure is formed by four attenuated A-shaped "fins" buttressed on each of the short sides of the plan. This allows the service floors to be structured in three large bays 86 ft (26 m) across (the distance between the shear walls) without any columns, enabling the internal spaces to be freely arranged.

The tower is horizontally divided into two large blocks, which are emphasized on the façade. The lower one, comprising 25 floors, will house offices, while the upper one is reserved for 47 floors of apartments, which will enjoy exclusive panoramic views. The crown of the building will have luxurious duplex and triplex penthouses, which will be the highest apartments in the world at the time of completion. An almost completely transparent triple-height sky-lobby is housed in the area separating the two blocks and acts as the entrance to a series of facilities for residents, including a reception for the 520 apartments, a lounge area, restaurants, and a health club with swimming pool. In addition to the 12 prestigious penthouses, future owners can choose from one-, two- or three-bedroom apartments.

The building will be entered through a spectacular quadruple-height foyer. Two main elevator cores serving the offices and the sky-lobby will be on the opposite sides of the tower. From the sky-lobby a small central elevator core will serve the residential floors.

119 top In this idealized image, you can view a representation of the entrance lobby. Note the seven supports for the transverse portals that, with almost 89 ft (27 m) between them, constitute the primary load-bearing system in this construction.

119 bottom This building welcomes visitors and residents through an impressive entrance lobby that is four levels high and has shops and commercial spaces, overlooking a lower level embellished with pools and planted areas.

The Index

An area of almost 65,000 sq ft (6,000 sq m) on the lower floors will house stores and commercial areas, while the basement will feature a parking lot with space for 2,681 vehicles.

Standing on a 215,000-sq-ft (20,000-sq-m) corner site, the tower will rise from a carefully landscaped plinth with ornamental pools. The building has an elongated plan with a rectangular base, orientated east–west to maximize views over the coastline and the desert, and also to reduce the effects of sunlight. Indeed, the northern façade is not directly exposed to the sun and the building core mass absorbs heat, reducing the energy required for mechanical ventilation. A system of sunshades shelters the interiors on the exposed south elevation. The project intends to maximize natural light and also features passive cooling systems for the interiors.   L.D.

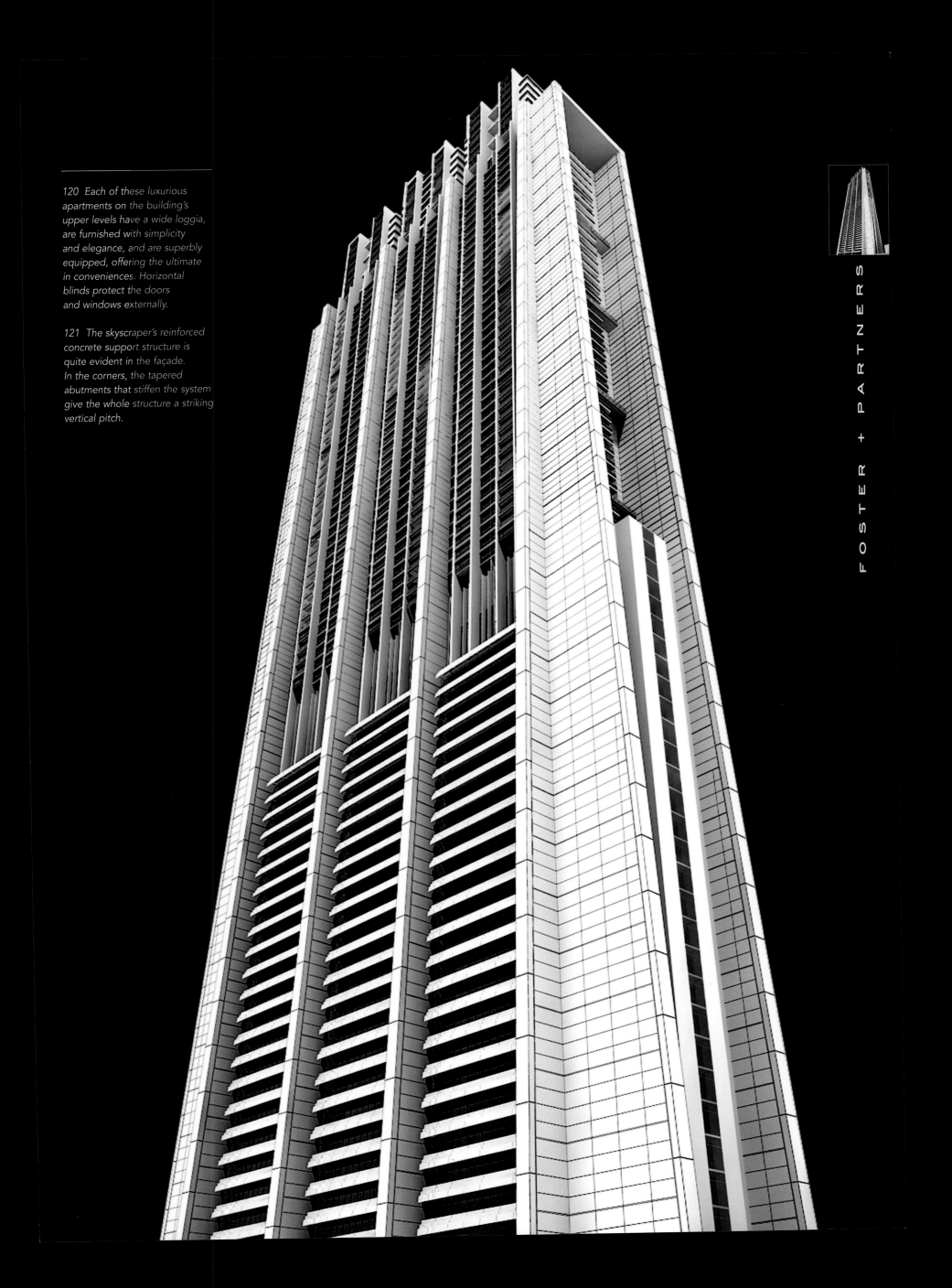

120 Each of these luxurious
apartments on the building's
upper levels have a wide loggia,
are furnished with simplicity
and elegance, and are superbly
equipped, offering the ultimate
in conveniences. Horizontal
blinds protect the doors
and windows externally.

121 The skyscraper's reinforced
concrete support structure is
quite evident in the façade.
In the corners, the tapered
abutments that stiffen the system
give the whole structure a striking
vertical pitch.

FOSTER + PARTNERS

Sun Tower

DUBAI

Even before realizing the actual function of the Dubai Sun Tower – designed in 2004 by Skidmore, Owings and Merrill LLP, but as yet unbuilt – the viewer will be impressed by its daring design. The structure is a rectangular-based tapering prism, which rises at an angle of 15 degrees, so that the top overhangs the base by 130 ft (40 m). This undeniably intriguing effect will be heightened by the building's location. It will stand on an isolated position in the center of a perfectly circular site almost completely surrounded by water, which has been created artificially by extending a stretch of the coastline into the sea.

However, the concept is not simply a virtuoso feat of construction, for the iconographic theme is very real: the tower is actually the gnomon of a huge sundial, mathematically calculated to show the time by projecting its shadow on the ground and the sea beyond. The layout of the plaza is based on these properties, with the green areas and urban furnishings designed to highlight significant shadow positions that mark the beginning and

end of the different seasons and the times of sunrise and sunset. The design evokes the local cultural tradition and is a tribute to Middle Eastern civilization, which conceived and employed the sundial thousands of years ago.

A hotel and residential units will occupy the lower half of the building, while the upper floors are destined for offices and service rooms. An observation deck and a restaurant will be located at the top. The building's structural function involves a central core formed by a staggered arrangement of blocks, housing the elevator shafts, and an external load-bearing cage consisting of perpendicular and sloping pillars. The sun will play a dual role in this building, for it not only allows the tower to show the time, but will also supply its energy requirements. Horizontal bands of solar panels will encase the tower, enabling the production of clean electricity with maximum efficiency, for there are no obstacles to their direct irradiation in the vicinity.

A lot of attention has been dedicated to constructional sustainability, which is also evident in the building's skin, which will be made from a double layer of glass. The space between the transparent panes will house a louvered shading system, which is adjusted automatically or by the occupants themselves as preferred. This will reduce solar gain and consequently also the amount of energy required for the air-conditioning of the interiors.

122 top From left, these blueprints illustrate the central nucleus of vertical connections, the spatial volume leaving open space for hanging gardens, the exterior structure of girders, and finally the grid frame for the curtain wall.

122 bottom In the vertical section highlighting the gradient incline of this structure, you can identify the diverse functional areas, the open space occupied by the hanging gardens, and the staggered line of vertical connections.

123 Representing the gnomon of a gigantic sundial, this building descends towards the sea. From the outside the structure will be a striking sight, while from inside it will have exclusive views of the Persian Gulf.

Sun Tower

Behind the façades, spaces will be carved out of the actual building to house hanging gardens on several levels. A further characteristic of the project is the greater structural dimensions of the floors destined to support the greater loads of the archive rooms.

The Dubai Sun Tower will stand out on the emirate's varied skyline because of its strong iconic image, rather than complex morphology or striking ornamental features. The building's simple geometry and clean lines, which represent an explicit engineering and technological challenge, will reproduce an ancient and highly evocative object on a giant scale.   L.D.

124-125 In this image, note the external double-pained glass enclosure with opaque strips of photovoltaic panels (providing a sustainable, clean source of energy for the building) and structural perimeter frame.

125 As illustrated by the floor plan, this skyscraper rises from an artificially created circular lot not 10 ft (3 m) from the shoreline. The shadow that signals the passage of time and the seasons projects onto the open area.

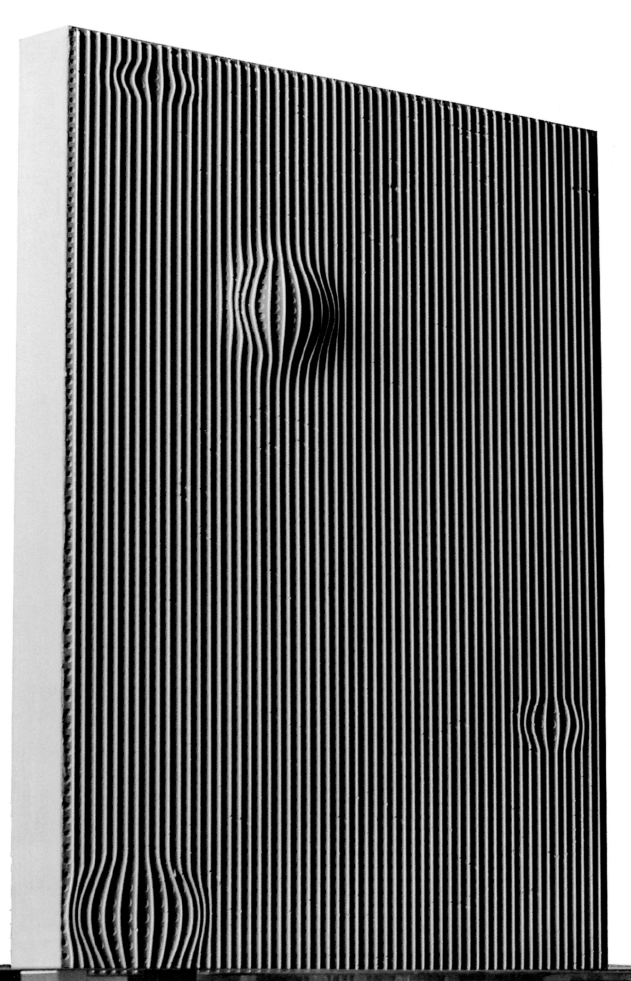

126 This monolith has a façade 656 ft (200 m) wide and 984 ft (300 m) high with a very simple design, based on a dense, impenetrable vertical division that at some points opens up and expands to accommodate lenticular projections.

127 The interior distribution of functions and in particular the hierarchical articulation of routes through the building reflect, in a vertical plane, the weft in the fabric of this historical city.

Dubai Renaissance

DUBAI

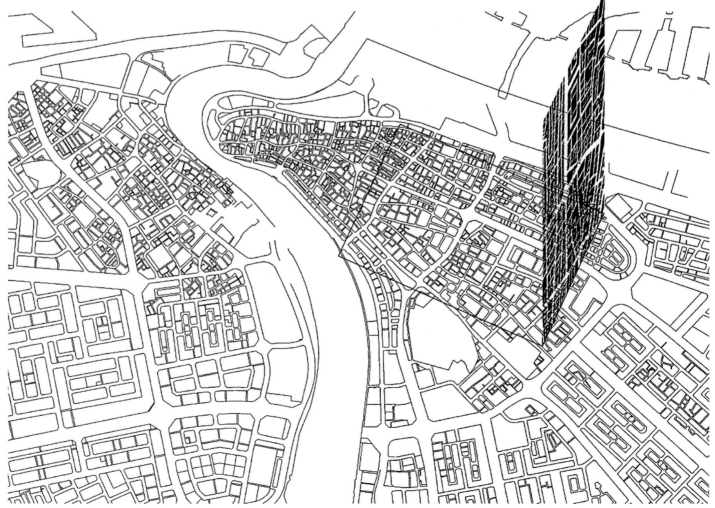

The Dubai Renaissance was the design entered by Rem Koolhaas' architectural firm OMA for a competition to design a multipurpose complex in the center of Dubai's newly expanded Business Bay district. Although first prize was won by Zaha Hadid's Dancing (now Signature) Towers, OMA is negotiating for the building's construction in another area of the city, near the Ras Al Khor Wildlife Sanctuary.

This building is emblematic of its designers' quest for architecture that offers an alternative to the contemporary individualism of the other competition entries, which are aimed at creating iconic buildings, distinctive even bizarre structures that stand out from their surroundings in order to promote themselves on the property market. The purity of form of Koolhaas' rectangular slab is intended to contrast it with the morphological arbitrariness of contemporary architecture and bring about a "renaissance" of the fundamental importance of the values of constructional, functional, and consequently aesthetic rationality.

However, its dimensions (660 ft/200 m long and 980 ft/300 m tall with a total area of 4.6 million sq ft/427,000 sq m) make the gigantic monolith so exceptional that it inevitably assumes an iconic, almost archetypal, significance. The approximate 10:1 ratio between the length of the building's main façade and its width means that it appears completely different from varying viewpoints: an enormous block on one side and an extremely slender tower on the other. In order to enhance this aspect, while avoiding the southern exposure and consequent excessive solar radiation of the façade with the largest area, the competition entry proposed building the structure on a huge revolving circular podium, but this concept was subsequently abandoned.

The functional mix offered by the mega-structure, comprising offices, a luxury hotel, private residences, business areas, and an underground parking lot, is organized rather like a city laid out on a verical grid. In the center of the building a core of elevators and stairs will allow access to the structure, serving three double-story lobbies at different levels.

These areas will house a Business Forum, a Wellness Lobby, and, on the top floor, a Panorama Lobby and all of them have uniquely designed interiors by Konstantin Grcic. From each of these lobbies it will be possible to reach two further elevator shafts, arranged symmetrically in relation to the main one, which will allow the single floors of each lobby to be accessed but will not serve street level or all the other floors of the building. This rational, if slightly cumbersome, system will enhance the public role of the lobbies.

The building's skin will be characterized by narrowly spaced vertical elements and a round swelling on one of the front façades, situated off-center about three quarters of the way up the structure, which will constitute the only interruption to the otherwise severely clean lines.   L.D.

128 and 129 In the initial proposal, the Dubai Renaissance building intended for Business Bay rotated on a vertical axis on a circular platform surrounded by water. This design would have moderated the impact of the building's size on the vicinity and would have offered its guests 360-degree views and a reduced requirement for air-conditioning. However, a claim for the reduction in energy consumption for air-conditioning must have been challenged because, according to the position of the sun, the shorter side would have been in direct contact with the sun's rays.

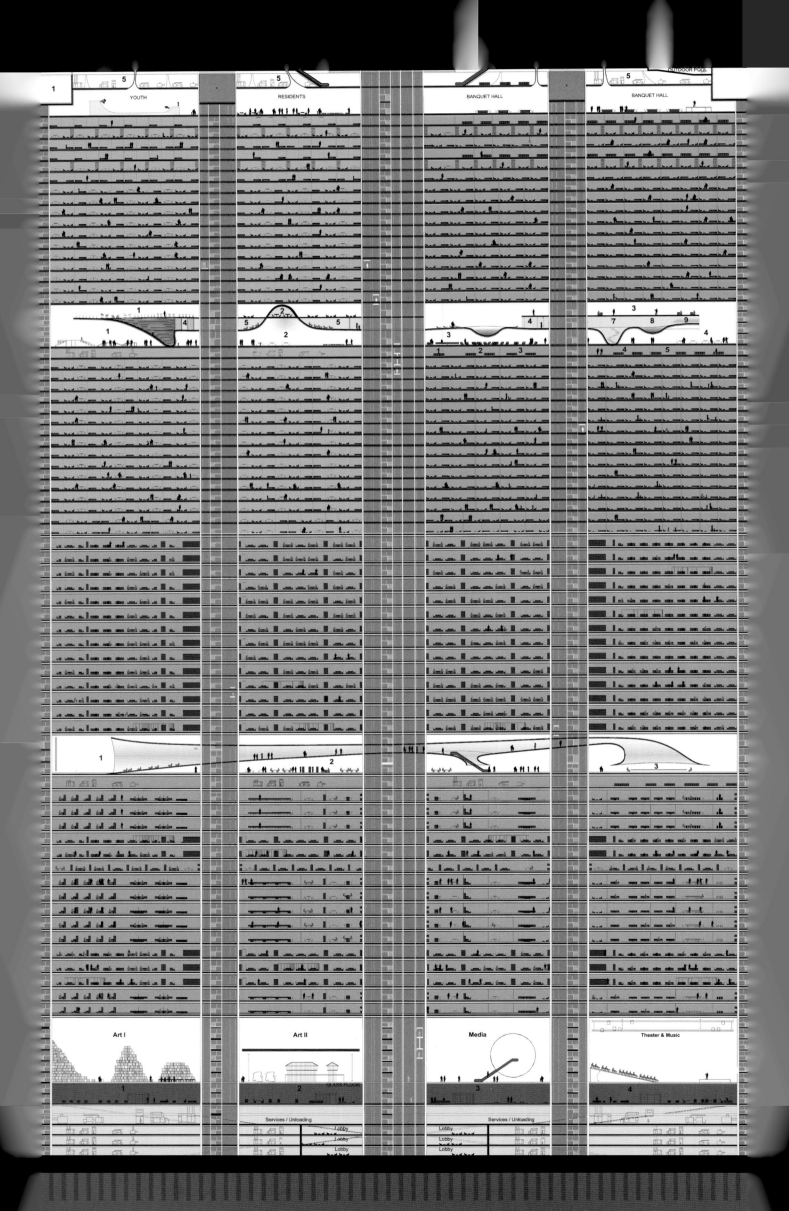

Dubai
Renaissance

130 The building's skeleton
emphasizes its functional
complexity and vertical nuclei
within the interior's spatial
distribution. You can also clearly
see the four large public spaces
on many levels.

131 This image illustrates
the interior spaciousness
of one of the public areas,
the Business Forum, and
a small 3D illustration of
a detail in its setup within
this section.

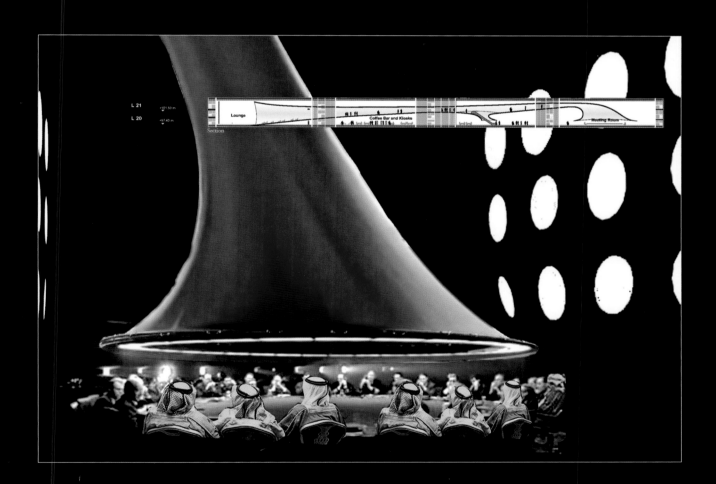

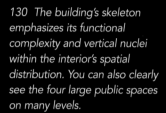

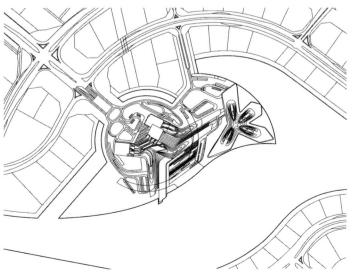

132-133 The Signature Towers occupy a lot at the center of the new expansion area of Business Bay, organized around a canal that enlarges a natural inlet.

132 bottom In the floor plan, representing a later elaboration to the initial project bid, skyscrapers rise up from the basement where the shape of the lower structures, housing commercial and recreational facilities, mirror the shape of the shadows made by the dominating towers.

133 Through a play on open and closed spaces, this façade shows a treatment that recaptures and emphasizes the motif of a skein of yarn, basing the entire architectural compositional dynamic on this theme.

Signature Towers

DUBAI

The Signature Towers will be one of the first high-rise buildings constructed by Zaha Hadid Associates that will fully realize the principles of their highly individual architectural idiom. The project was the winner of a design competition held in 2005/06 by Dubai Properties, in which other leading names of international architecture, such as OMA, Reiser and Umemoto, and Morphosis, were also invited to participate. They all produced such interesting designs that they will be adapted for other projects.

Zaha Hadid uses fluid, flexible dynamic lines to interpret and translate the functional complexity and physical density of the contemporary metropolis. In the design for this multipurpose complex, the British-Iraqi architect's style is interpreted through the image of a bundle of tubes or filaments. According to the writings of Patrik Schumacher, a partner of the firm, the aim of the project – which explicitly seeks to update of the "Fordist" skyscraper based on the repetitive uniformity of stories, and the isolated tower distanced from its surroundings by an emblematic base or podium – can be summed up in three keywords. These are differentiation, intended as the variety of forms distinguishing each high-rise building; interface, denoting the attempt to engage and link with the ground plan; and navigation, referring to the multiple methods of penetration, circulation and perception of inner spaces.

In the Dubai project, which will be the focus of the new Business Bay development (220 new high-rise buildings along a canal extending the famous Creek), the three towers will translate sideways at different angles, intertwining and intersecting to form an irregular silhouette accentuated by the bundled arrangement of the lines of the façades, hence the highly appropriate original name of "dancing towers." This "choreography," for which Arup are the structural, engineering, and safety consultants, is arranged in such a way that the buildings will shade each other from the hot Dubai sun, helping to keep their occupants comfortable, and reflect the specific functions of the various areas. Each of the three towers are destined for a particular use: the office tower will be connected on the ground to the hotel tower, which in turn will be linked at the top to the residential tower in order to share service and maintenance functions. In the podium, structures built on plans following the shadow of the towers will house recreational and commercial facilities for all residents, while the underground levels will house technical services and parking lots. This spatial symbiosis aims to create a mixed-use structure and allows complex and varied forms of utilization in which the interiors will be lively throughout the entire day.

The formal and functional dynamism is extended to relate to a series of public spaces in the surrounding area, and consequently with the rest of the city. In the competition entry, the circular site on which the buildings stand, isolated from the rest of the development by a road running around its perimeter, was connected via a bridge to a park to the east, while a second bridge with separate levels for traffic and pedestrians, crossed the canal to the west. In the subsequent drafts the park is shown next to the towers, while the connection to the opposite bank of the canal is achieved by way of a structure overhanging the water.   L.D.

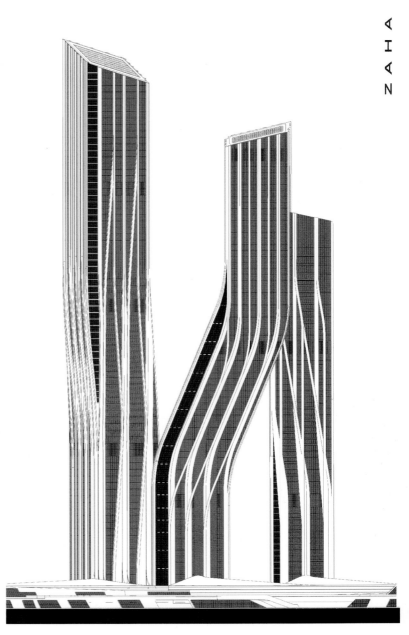

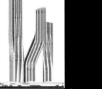

134 The towers are an integral part of a complex system of access points and routes that include the road and pedestrian traffic networks, easily distinguishable in a night-time setting.

134-135 The towers' interior atria reach almost the full height of the building, creating an interior space that has great impact in explicit homage to John Portmann's invention of the skyscraper.

136 The angle and position of these skyscrapers in relation to the orientation of the lot on which they were constructed was studied in depth in order to guarantee the maximum amount of mutual shading to counter excessive solar gain.

136-137 Each of these skyscrapers have a different role. However, the offices on the right side of the image are connected via the ground floor to the hotel which in turn links to the residential building to share common functions.

138-139 This complex is built from a base of six floors for commercial use with five towers of diverse height emerging from it, which house offices, residential units, and a hotel.

138 bottom This settlement is located in a northwestern area of Al Reem Island. The entire area of about 1,564 acres (633 hectares) is the object of an urban development plan that will accommodate 280,000 people.

139 On the lower levels, atria and open spaces covered with sheet-metal awnings afford shade from the sun and provide passive cooling to an area rich with vegetation.

Eco Bay

ABU DHABI

The city of Abu Dhabi is situated on one of the coastal islands that are a geographical feature of the area. Its rapid urban expansion has now extended to encompass the shore of the nearby mainland, as well as other islands that can be easily linked by bridges, due to the commercial desirability of property with access to the sea and a waterfront position. The Eco Bay complex is part of the larger Al Reem Island project, developed separately by Sorouh, Reem Investments, and Tamouh. The mixed-use complex will cover the entire area of Al Reem Island and will be able to house 280,000 people. The natural island covers an area of approximately 2.5 sq miles (6.5 sq km) and is currently almost deserted, except for a huge private mansion.

The project was designed by the London architecture firm Llewelyn Davies Yeang in conjunction with its Kuala Lumpur affiliate T.R. Hamzah and Yeang. They won the first prize in a competition held by Sorouh in which seven carefully selected international firms were invited to submit entries for the construction of a mixed-use complex on a plot of four million sq ft (370,000 sq m) near the island's north coast. The project consists of a six-story base for commercial use, from which five towers will rise. Two of the towers will house offices, two will have residential units, and one a hotel.

Ken Yeang, the Malaysian-born architect who heads both firms, is famous for his "bioclimatic" design concept, which is an ecological approach to the construction of skyscrapers that he pioneered and has developed over the years through various projects, publications, and university lectures. His solution for Abu Dhabi represents a further step in his bioclimatic quest and is presented as a third alternative for the typological and distributional organization of mixed-use developments in hot, arid countries, where prolonged outdoor activity is impossible for many months of the year. Commercial and public areas are generally either housed inside buildings accessed directly from the street or enclosed in climate-controlled malls. The Eco Bay project, on the other hand, is based on the idea of a "green oasis of ecological living." A network of passively cooled gardens and public spaces that cover the entire complex, connected both horizontally and vertically.

The close-woven layout of the Islamic city, which widens into shady spaces or tree-planted courtyards, is literally transposed vertically in these skyscrapers, which will be home to hanging gardens with lush green vegetation on different levels, and this will be echoed in the multistory base with full-height spaces, atriums, and plazas that will allow the natural light and greenery to penetrate even the areas below ground. Canopies will protect the open spaces not shaded by the buildings, while the solar chimney effect created in the atriums and the updrafts from the opposite north and south façades will ensure the natural ventilation of the outdoor areas. The plants will not only embellish the complex, but will also humidify the atmosphere, lowering the temperature and improving the microclimate. This green system, which will be visible on the façade through the transparent parts of the skin and on the roofs, is also the key to the composition of the entire complex and is made even more evident by the simple linear design of the façades.   L.D.

LLEWELYN DAVIES YEANG T.R. HAMZAH & YEANG SDN. BHD.

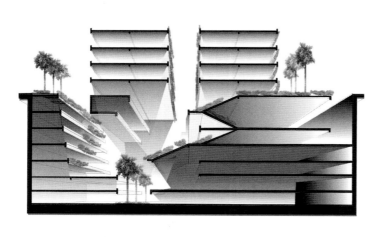

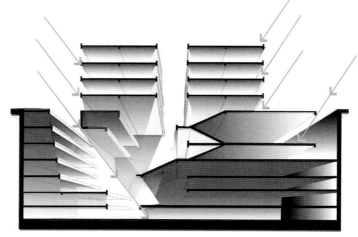

140-141 In this construction elevation, green spaces are quite visible in various areas, characterizing a distinctive element of formal, simple, and linear architectural language.

140 bottom This vertical section of offices highlights how the connection between the atria on several levels allows natural zenithal light into the interiors and in the basement.

LLEWELYN DAVIES YEANG T.R.
HAMZAH & YEANG SDN. BHD.

141 bottom left This plan illustrates the green oasis concept of ecological living, with its system of atria, interior public areas, and vertical connections where rich vegetation grows within a passive cooling spatial system.

141 bottom right The green interior gardens contribute to lowering the temperature whether due to increased humidity or ventilation from the chimney effect produced in the atria throughout the building.

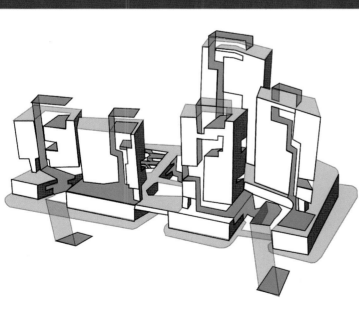

Khaledya
ABU DHABI

The Khaledya Tower is a project designed by Sybarite, a London-based firm of young architects who broke away from Future Systems in 2002. Their hallmark philosophy is to combine functionality with sensual pleasure, creating alluring, highly original works that seamlessly blend art, sculpture, and architecture. This particular building, designed for a long narrow site in central Abu Dhabi, will have a striking curved sculptural form, inspired by the natural landscape of desert dunes, but interpreted through the style of industrial design applied to everyday objects, such as crash helmets The project nonetheless seems to satisfy all the necessary requirements for such a building in terms of use and construction.

This distinctive building will be 328 ft (100 m) high and its main façades will be concave while the short sides convex, creating striking vistas from below. The building's geometric form is derived from an egg-shaped solid, symmetrically carved out on two opposite sides. It will be set in a sunken garden below street level.

142 and 143 This building takes a form derived from an ovoid space hollowed out on two opposite symetrical façades. The main façades result in a concave shape, while the lateral façades are convex. Due to their differing curvatures, the shiny surfaces of the glassed exterior enclosure create evocative effects as they reflect the surrounding environment. Honeycomb siding also provides a shading system.

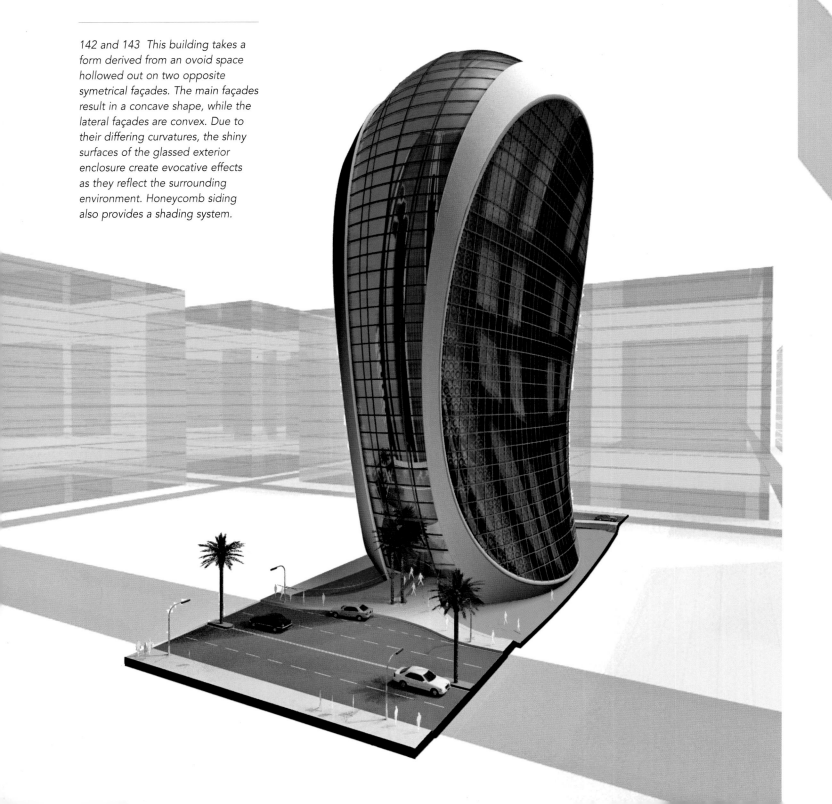

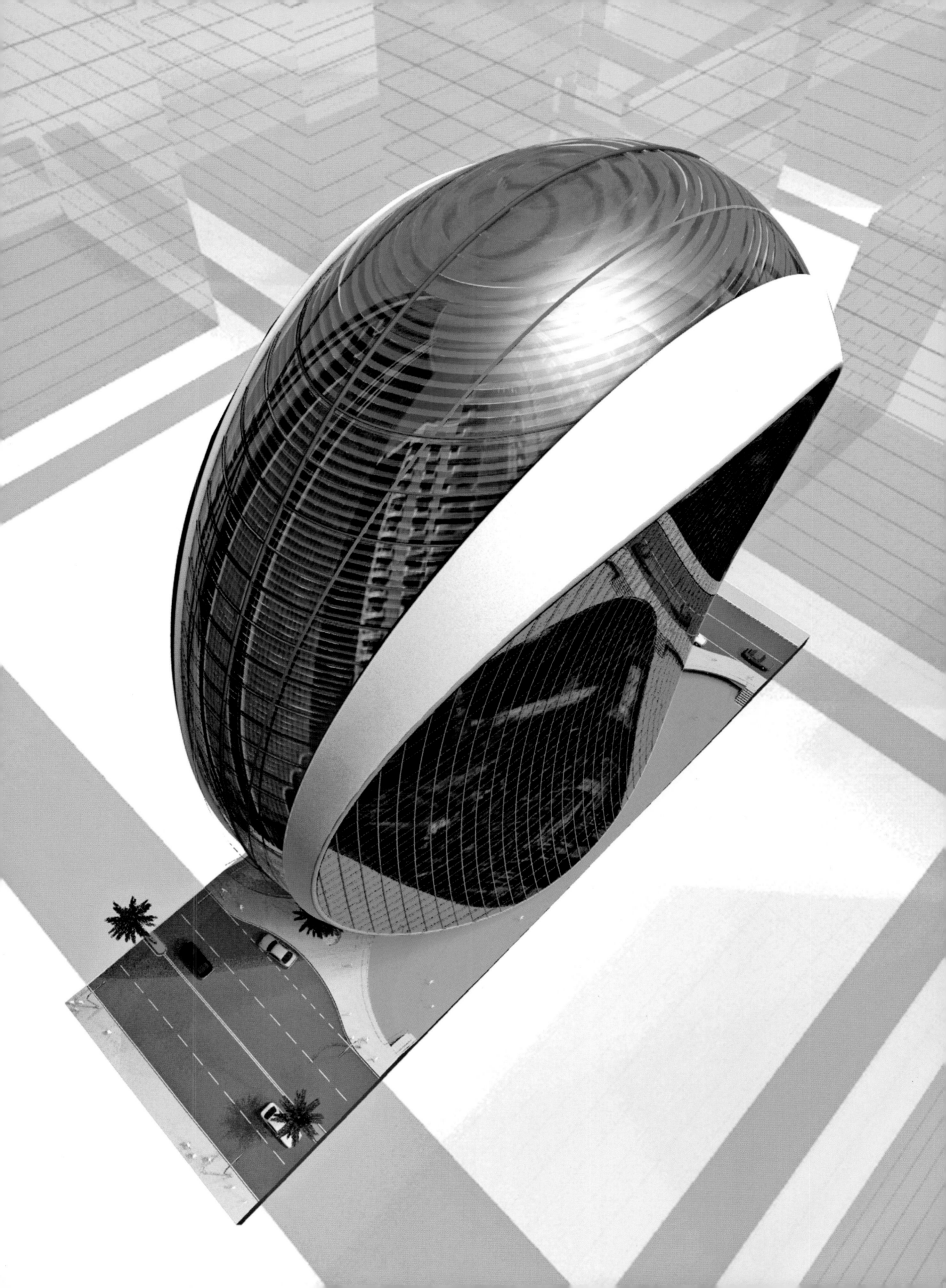

Khaledya

The raised entrance will be accessed via two identical curved pedestrian walkways from the streets running along the short sides of the site. A central rectangular core, which will house bathrooms and elevator shafts and stairwells, will serve all 18 floors of the building, providing a total area of around 215,000 sq ft (20,000 sq m) for offices, residential units, and commercial premises. Inside the faceted glass skin, shaded from the sun by honeycombed louvers, curved pillars will be regularly spaced along the concave sides of the building to support the floors (consequently, the floor areas will vary according to height), forming a structure strengthened by two large reinforced concrete rings visible on the façade. The basement floors will have a parking lot with a total area of almost 50,000 sq ft (4,600 sq m).   L.D.

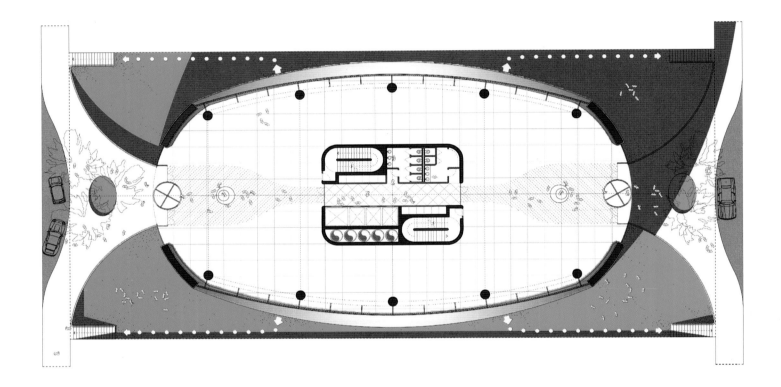

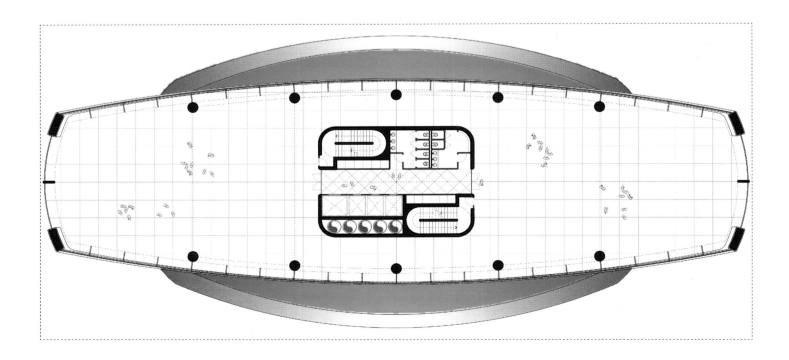

144 top One floor above street level, the entrance is accessible through two double symmetrical walkways. Four staircases at the highest part of the lot descend from the street to the lower garden in the remaining open area.

144 bottom The building's design varies in proportion on each level. By confining the overall structural dimensions to the perimeter and central core of vertical connections, this allows the distribution of ample open areas in the floor plan.

145 The hollowing out of the symmetrical lateral facings is evident, creating as it does concave façade surfaces. Note the two reinforced concrete rings that stiffen the structure and, in the center, the walkway access point.

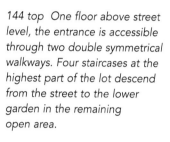

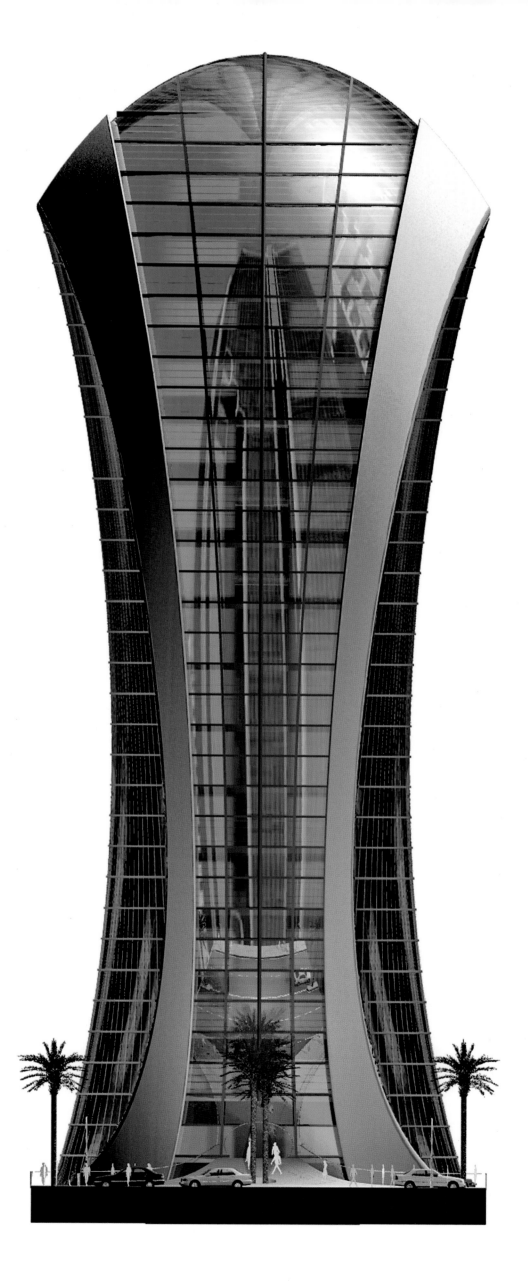

The Opus

DUBAI

Designed by Zaha Hadid Associates, The Opus is a futuristic mixed-use building, destined to house mainly executive offices. It will be situated in Dubai's Business Bay and will engage visually with a series of other iconic structures, such as the Burj Khalifa and the Signature Towers, along the lines set out by the master plan that regulates the development of this strategic district. Construction of The Opus is due to be completed in 2010.

The design of the building is a huge crystal cube, which has been transformed by carving out a fluid void to create the unstable geometric forms that characterize Hadid's work. The void seems to corrode the compact block, dividing it into three 305-ft (92-m) tall towers. This empty space is treated as a volume in its own right, which paradoxically defines the form of the actual cube. The interior of the void will be clad with an innovative curved glass curtain-wall system, allowing stunning views and differentiating the internal façades from the rest of the skin, as the light is reflected off them at different angles. The effect will be to heighten the contrast between the free form of the void and the external image of the rest of

146-147 *Although the building appears to be one large parallelepiped of glass, in reality it is composed of two distinct structural bodies connected near the entrance atrium and rooftop suspended bridge.*

147 *The eventual construction of the Opus in Business Bay, a strategic part of this city, will establish a physical and spatial relationship with some of the most innovative buildings, such as the Burj Khalifa and Signature Tower.*

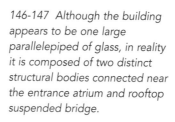

building. The inner base of the central void will house areas for recreation and relaxation.

Although conceived as a single solid volume, which appears as a cube suspended above the ground due to the transparent glass walls of the ground floor, the building will actually consist of two distinct blocks, connected via the atrium, the gallery on the first three levels, and a sky bridge between the top floors. The lobby that will welcome visitors and house several luxurious boutiques is arranged on two levels connected by escalators and has been conceived as an open space in which multiple paths and flows of people will cross. This part of the building opens onto all four sides of the block in order to maximize accessibility. The galleries on the upper floors are reached via the lobby. They will have stores and Omniyat Properties' innovative Oyster concept, including a gym, Tranquillity Zone, and other services intended mainly for guests, who will be able to alternate work with relaxation. Like the stores on the third gallery level, these areas are arranged in a ring around a central core housing elevator shafts and stairwells that will be lit through the glass skin surrounding the void.

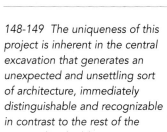

148-149 The uniqueness of this project is inherent in the central excavation that generates an unexpected and unsettling sort of architecture, immediately distinguishable and recognizable in contrast to the rest of the surrounding buildings.

150 and 150-151 The large open space, whose fluid form seems to expand beyond the physical boundaries of the standard cube, was produced with a single piece of curved glass in a continuous transparent wall, stretching smoothly around the construction.

Allowing spectacular views of Dubai's Business Bay, this glass wrap also shields the interior from unwelcome observation from neighboring offices. The building's original form and structure becomes increasingly apparent at night.

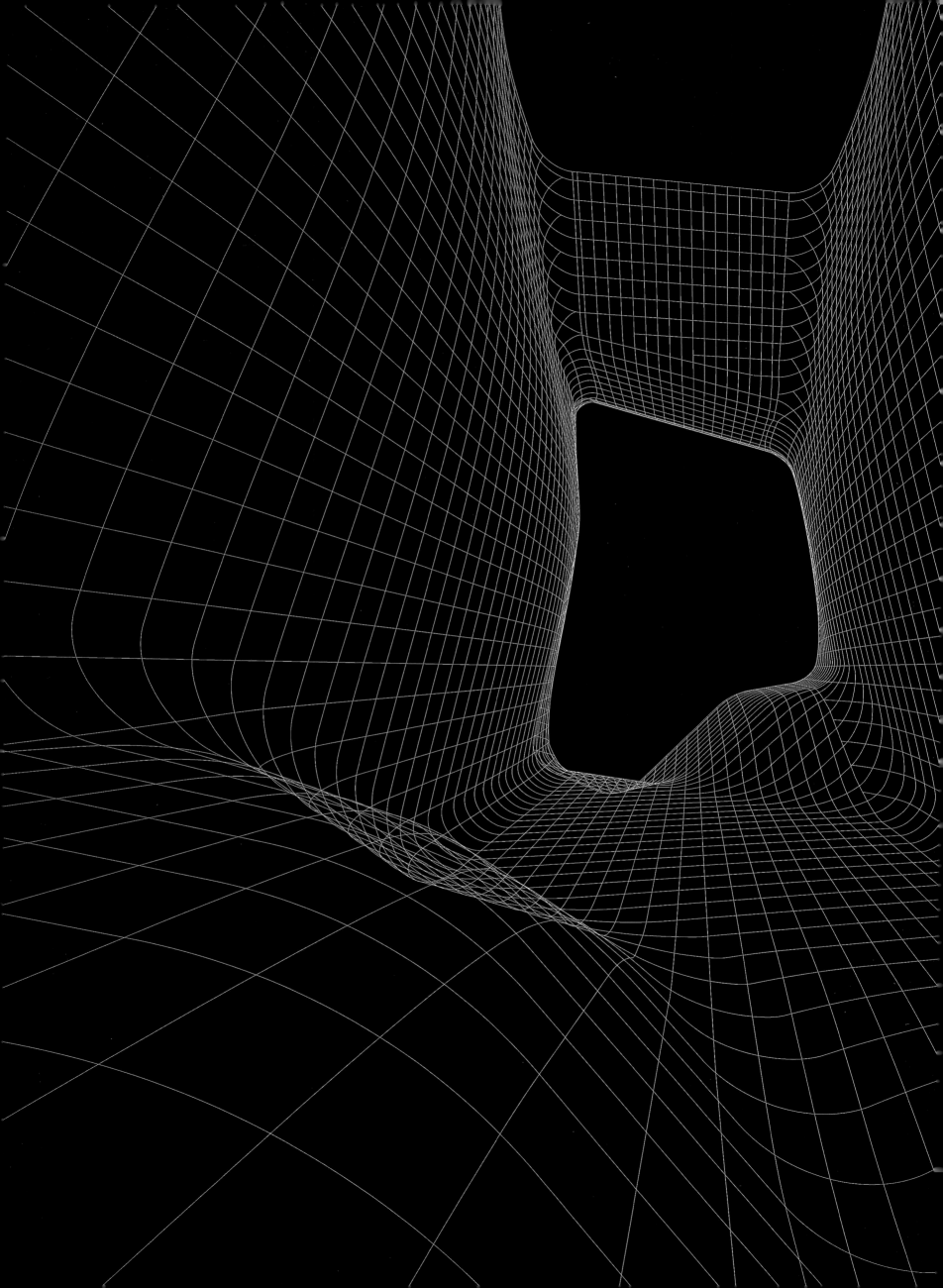

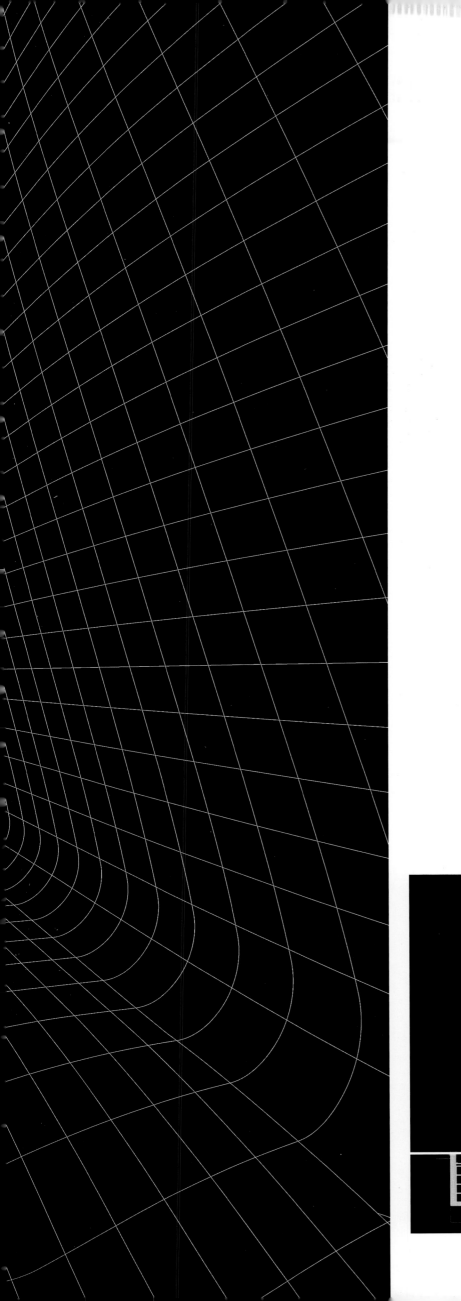

Above the gallery will be 18 floors of offices, designed to exploit the floor space to the full and maximize flexibility. This is achieved by positioning the block housing elevator shafts and stairwells in the center of the towers, while the pillars are slightly set back from the perimeter of the building.

Particular attention has been paid to the design of the structure's skin, which will be made from glass with reflective patterns in the form of pixelated striations, which will moderate the massivness of the cube while controlling natural light and heat from the sun. The building has been designed to generate different effects at different times of day. During daylight hours the main volume will appear full and solid, in spite of the void, which will seem to disappear, while at night the cube will appear dark and dematerialized, in contrast to the illuminated void, which will be visible from afar.

Another distinctive feature of the building is its energy-saving design. It has been conceived to challenge the traditional idea of the office block, in terms of both its amazing geometry and its high environmental sustainability, which will be achieved using state-of-the-art construction technologies.   O.E.B.

152-153 3D modelling for this project served mainly to define the form of the interior spaces in order to establish their dimensions, metaphorical effect, and spatial character.

153 This building is composed of 22 floating floors, anchored to the ground through a subterranean basement excavated to include a large parking area distributed over five levels.

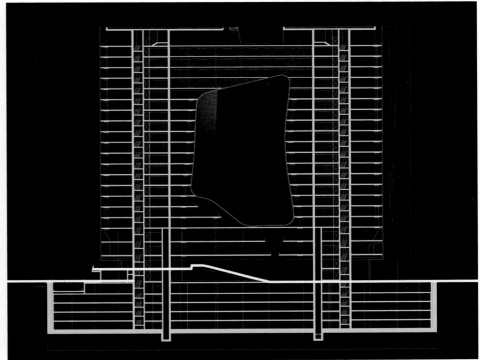

154-155 and 155 These interiors recapture the theoretical principles that brought definition to its form and structure, resulting in the fluid yet unsettling geometry typical of Zaha Hadid's architecture. Changing flooring levels, long mobile staircases, and slightly sloping ramps entwine with walls, lowered ceilings, and furnishings with soft and graceful lines whose dynamic nature is highlighted by the light that filters through the large perimeter windows.

arkan architects-consultants (bay

partners (jumeirah beach hotel - burj al a

sybarite (apeiron island hotel) - sanjay

hotels

unah hilton tower hotel) - ws atkins &
b) - ateliers jean nouvel (w hotel) -
uri architects (eta hotel)

hotels

During the 1990s, influenced by the foresight of Sheikh Zayed, the sheikhs of the UAE agreed on the need to develop new economic sectors unrelated to the exploitation of oil resources. They thus commissioned imposing and futuristic hotel buildings from some of the world's largest and most renowned architecture firms, which allowed them to establish the country as a leading luxury tourist destination in the space of just a few years. Indeed, a large number of all the buildings erected in the new Middle Eastern metropolises are hotel and tourist facilities. Dubai alone currently offers over 40,000 hotel rooms and furnished apartments of various categories and is planning to increase the figure by 50 percent within the next year, becoming the city with the greatest number of accommodation facilities per square mile in the world. The country's capital, Abu Dhabi,

also offers a wide range of excellent hotels. Together with Sharjah, it presents itself as a destination for cultural tourists, attracted by its museums and art itineraries, as well as business visitors, as it is one of the favorite bases for banks and financial companies.

Although tourism-related property development is at its most advanced and dynamic in Dubai and Abu Dhabi, the five other emirates are also developing an extensive infrastructure system and showing great prospects for growth. However, these new construction projects are designed to respect the character of their locations, and thus are aimed at people interested in the sea, natural beauties, history, and local traditions. Tourism is almost exclusively concentrated on the coast, which attracts visitors who come for the crystal-clear waters and white sandy beaches, as well as for the spectacular buildings.

One of the earliest and most important developments is Jumeirah Beach in Dubai, where the hotel chain owned by the Al Maktoum family has built four of the most splendid structures. These include the Burj Al Arab, which has become an international icon of luxury due to its self-ascribed seven stars (although only five of these are officially recognized, in accordance with international hotel rating systems). The building, designed by Tom Wright for London-based W. S. Atkins, is undoubtedly the most overused image of all the buildings in the Gulf region and represents the new trends in hotel architecture in the UAE. Luxury, magnificence, exclusiveness, originality, maximum comfort, variety, and international cuisine are just some of the features shared by almost all the hotels. The structures offer various services, from luxury shopping to numerous leisure opportunities, state-of-the-art spa treatments and exclusive sports facilities. Regardless of their category, all the hotels boast supremely high standards with exceptionally comfortable, fully air-conditioned rooms equipped with the very latest technology.

An efficient and constantly developing infrastructure system (including Dubai's first subway line) connects all the hotels, which are easily reached from the existing airports and the larger ones that are already planned to deal with the expected tourism boom. An example is the Dubai World Central International Airport, which will be the largest and busiest airport in the world, able to handle far more than the current 17 million passengers transiting through the emirate and due to be completed within ten years.

Over the years, the projects commissioned from the leading architecture firms have gradually become more and more daring, spectacular, complex, and technologically advanced. The visual impact of these structures is based on the amazement evoked by their highly innovative forms, thanks to a sort of contest to create the most surprising building. Three artificial archipelagos arranged in the form of palm trees with hotels and private homes for rich holidaymakers, are due to be completed by 2015 off the coast of Dubai. They will be joined by The World, 300 islands reproducing a map of the world, currently under construction with prices ranging from 1 to 15 million U.S. dollars.

The most recent projects, still at the design stage, are of apparently impossible buildings, which rise out of the waters of the Persian Gulf or dematerialize behind their façades. The world's leading architects are currently building structures unrivalled anywhere in the world. Inspiration for the forms of these building is drawn chiefly from the country's well-established seafaring and merchant traditions, for example, the dhows and their large wind-filled sails. Indeed, the Jumeirah Beach Hotel, which reflects the waters of the Gulf, has the form of a wave, while the shape of a hull is equally evident in Jean Nouvel's W Hotel and in the Hilton Baynunah in Abu Dhabi. The recurrent themes that influence the projects are implicit in the incessant development of new systems to improve the energy efficiency of the buildings and the constant quest to find the ideal balance of technological innovation and local tradition. The latter is the source for both the figurative themes of the structures and the natural cooling systems of their interiors. O.E.B.

Baynunah Hilton Tower Hotel

ABU DHABI

The 42-story Hilton Baynunah Hotel rises above the skyscrapers of the Abu Dhabi skyline to a height of over 540 ft (165 m). Designed by Arkan Architects-Consultants, it is situated on the handsome Abu Dhabi Corniche, about a mile from the city center and close to the city's main tourist, cultural, and commercial attractions, such as the Abu Dhabi Mall, Madina Zayed, Gold Souk, and Bedouin Heritage Village.

Completed in February 1995, the Baynunah Tower marked a shift away from the city's traditional building styles in favor of innovative new structures. At the time, it was not only the tallest and most prestigious tower in the whole of Abu Dhabi, but also the first building to have been built from silica-fume concrete, which ensures excellent durability and resistance in extreme climates, such as that of the Persian Gulf. The reinforced concrete structural frame is built on pile foundations with a diameter ranging from 31 to 43 inches (78–110 cm), while the skin is formed by a simple glass curtain wall.

The tower has a complex form, composed of three structures with a total area of 485,000 sq ft (45,000 sq m). Each of these three structures has a different elevation and a different number of stories (25, 31, and 37), and is arranged around a fourth central structure with 42 floors and a cylindrical form that houses the elevator shafts, stairwells, and water tanks. The result is an austere and original building, whose formal appearance and setting conjure up images of a great flagship.

160 top The articulation of space here is rather complex, but easily interpreted when observed from the park alongside the Abu Dhabi Corniche.

160 bottom These façades and sections clarify the proportions of the complex. Differing heights in the glass-windowed towers were chosen based on an attempt at dimensional harmony among the

various parts, while cylindrical turrets contribute to defining the figurative appearance and emphasizing a chromatic characterization of the components.

161 A fourth space completes the structure. Eight levels with façades in blue glass, a massive crown, and vertical reinforced concrete elements separating the façades define this building.

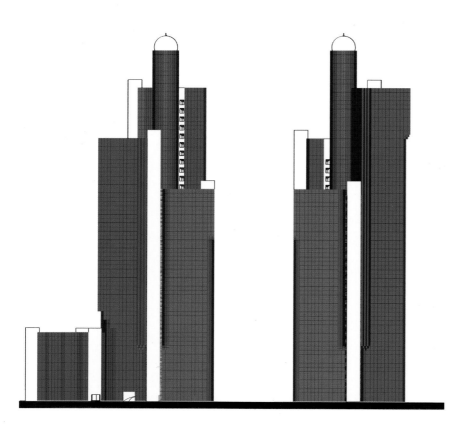

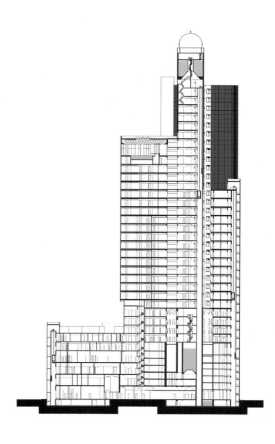

162 top The inner city site of the Baynunah Tower is strategic. At not even 1.25 miles (2 km) from downtown, it stands sentry at the waterfront of the picturesque Abu Dhabi Corniche quarter in an area that is full of tourist attractions, parks, and other public facilities.

162 bottom The floor plan of this building results from the triangular shape of the lot. Three principal tower structures are arranged in radial symmetry around the cylindrical turret that rises to 42 floors in height, holding the primary vertical connections. Other smaller circular towers, housing elevator machinery, complete the construction.

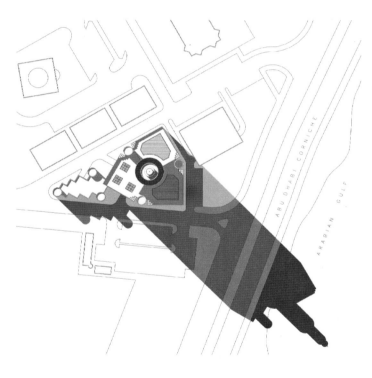

162-163 The patterned enclosure covering the height of the cylindrical turrets is not straightforward, but characterized by a geometric bas relief pattern in an Islamic decorative style.

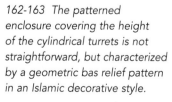

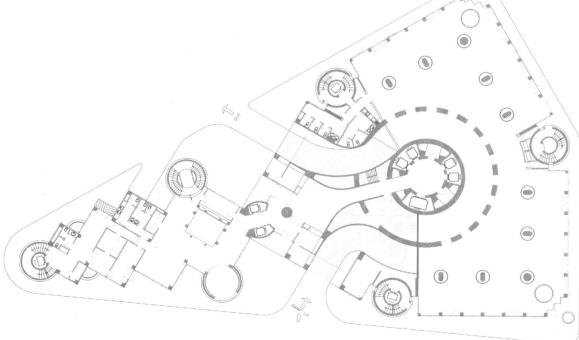

While this figurative metaphor is undoubtedly less romantic than that of the dhow, evoked in the architectural forms of other buildings in the United Arab Emirates, it is equally effective in emphasizing a symbolic link between the structure and the waters of the Gulf. The outer skin is formed predominantly of dark blue glass, which encases the three structures, characterizing the nature and appearance of the building, while the slim cylindrical towers are clad with ornamental concrete panels.

Huge quantities of imported marble and granite have been used for the floors and walls of the sumptuous interiors. The ground floor not only houses the atrium and reception, but also a shopping mall with many stores and boutiques. A six-story parking lot is available for guests. A heated indoor swimming pool is located on the 29th floor, on the roof of the second structure at a height of 331 ft (100 m). Its floor-to-ceiling windows offer spectacular views over the city and the sea. The Hilton Baynunah also boasts a gym, a beauty salon, bars, restaurants, and a business center able to seat 150 people. The hotel's 139 luxurious spacious rooms offer all the amenities that one would expect from this hotel chain, while the 86 deluxe suites of various sizes all boast a kitchenette and panoramic views over Abu Dhabi and the Persian Gulf.   O.E.B.

164-165 Designed by WS Atkins & Partners, this hotel rises above the white sand of Jumeirah Beach and stretches out along the coast, just over 9 miles (14.5 km) from Dubai.

164 bottom Next to the hotel, the famous Dubai Wild Wadi Water Park expands over an area of almost 10 acres (4 hectares), offering numerous attractions and countless hours of fun that draw many tourists, and where it is also possible to enjoy beautiful views of the Burj Al Arab.

165 top The glass enclosure that almost completely covers the vertical surfaces of the Jumeirah Beach Hotel is covered by a second opaque sheath, articulated with square apertures that modulate the sun's rays into the lower level spaces.

165 bottom In space, form, and materials, the Jumeirah Beach Hotel proves to have a close relationship with the more famous Dubai Burj Al Arab, the ultimate seven-star luxury hotel and icon of the Dubai skyline, also designed by Atkins for the hotel chain owned by the Al Maktum family.

Jumeirah Beach Hotel

DUBAI

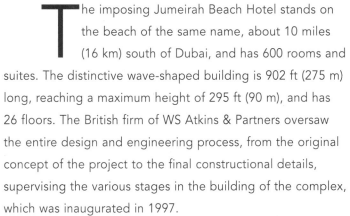

The imposing Jumeirah Beach Hotel stands on the beach of the same name, about 10 miles (16 km) south of Dubai, and has 600 rooms and suites. The distinctive wave-shaped building is 902 ft (275 m) long, reaching a maximum height of 295 ft (90 m), and has 26 floors. The British firm of WS Atkins & Partners oversaw the entire design and engineering process, from the original concept of the project to the final constructional details, supervising the various stages in the building of the complex, which was inaugurated in 1997.

The hotel's position and role within a much larger master plan place it in close visual relation with another structure with unusual dimensions and characteristics, the famous seven-star Burj Al Arab hotel, which was built two years later by the same architects and has become the internationally recognized symbol of the new Dubai. The sail-like tower is situated exactly opposite the Jumeirah Beach Hotel. Next to the hotel is Dubai's famous Wild Wadi Water Park, which is also part of the development plan drawn up for this stretch of coast.

The symbolic concept of the Jumeirah Beach Hotel was devised by its architects to emphasize the building's bond with the waters of the Persian Gulf. Indeed, the form of the structure conjures up several marine metaphors: the dorsal fin of a sea creature, silhouetted against the landscape as though linking sea and sky; the sail of a dhow, the traditional lateen-rigged ship of the region; or an ocean wave about to break against the shore.

166 Observed in a parallel
perspective to the coast, the
spatial body of the building loses
its massive appearance and
demonstrates a fluidity in form,
revealing an unexpected
lightness in design.

167 The curvilinear northern
gable accommodates the rooms'
individual terraces. Due to their
particular position and variable
angle, one can enjoy a panoramic
view from every one of them, with
each terrace varying in design.

168 This hotel's luxurious interiors are enhanced by imported marble and granite, high quality fabrics, and modern style decor. The hotel is also equipped for meetings and receptions.

168-169 This structure includes several panoramic restaurants that offer both local and international cuisine to satisfy the demands of all customers.

170-171 The atrium is more than 295 ft (90 m) high and corridors open off it on various levels, leading to rooms located in the two wings of the building. A large wall decoration embellishes the space, using LED lighting to depict the earth, sun, and moon. Bright colors are repeated in the variegated shades of the flooring and furnishings.

Both the plan and the elevation of the hotel have a sinuous, fluid design that recalls the ebb and flow of the sea. The unbroken reflective glass skin gives the building an impalpable appearance, which merges its fluid silhouette with the sea and vice versa. Consequently, despite the building's impressive size, which makes it visible for miles around, its true form can only be distinguished at close quarters.

The complex is comprised of two different triangular "wings," anchored to a reinforced concrete structural core that houses elevator shafts and stairwells and the entrance, and leads to an atrium occupying the entire height of the

building (over 295 ft/90 m), whose upper part is decorated with an enormous satellite view of the earth, with the moon and a red sun. The lobby leads to a spectacular two-tiered colonnade that forms a graceful 400-ft (122-m) curve along the beach side of the hotel, passing shop windows and a large external courtyard planted with palm trees. Guests can relax around the pool, enjoying magnificent sea views from the terrace overlooking the beach.

Accessed from a corridor on the opposite side of the building to the beach, and consequently all overlooking the sea, each of the rooms has a slightly different view, due to

the sinuous design of the complex. The decor is based on the theme of the four natural elements: earth, water, air, and fire. In order to avoid disturbing guests and intruding on the hotel's architectural image, the massive cooling plant required for the air-conditioning of the complex is located over a quarter of a mile away, in a lozenge-shaped structure reminiscent of the keel of a dhow which also houses a conference center, a ballroom, a banqueting hall, and an auditorium.

A sports club is situated at the far end of the complex, overlooking a marina formed by two elegant breakwaters. O.E.B.

172 top South of the hotel, a rhomboid-shaped building holds a conference center, ballroom, and banquet room with all associated services available. This facility is separate from the hotel but the sinuous design of its exterior spaces follows the same architectural profile of the primary building.

172 bottom Shown in this night-time scene is the hotel's outdoor pool and exterior green spaces. It is also possible to glimpse the marina's wharf in the background.

172-173 Accommodating the conference center, this building's design is clearly inspired by the shapes and materials of sailboats that navigate the waters of the Persian Gulf.

174-175 The design of the Jumeirah Beach Hotel is clearly inspired by the shape of a large wave. Reflections and transparency effects visible during the night give special emphasis to the lightweight glass enclosure and to its contrast with other opaque finishes. In a play of chiaroscuro, the hotel's silhouette diminishes as it reflects on the calm waters of the Gulf.

Burj Al Arab

DUBAI

The seven-star Burj Al Arab ("Tower of the Arabs") is not only one of the world's most luxurious hotels and one of the most emblematic silhouettes on the Dubai skyline, but is also among the most recognizable icons of international architecture, despite the fact that the more recent spectacular buildings of the Emirates have now beaten its many records. Situated on Jumeirah Beach, about 10 miles (16 km) south of Dubai, construction of the 1053-ft (320-m) tall hotel was commenced in 1994 on a custom-built artificial island 919 ft (280 m) off the coast in order to ensure the privacy of its guests. The island is connected to the mainland by a bridge suspended above the waters of the Persian Gulf, although a helipad on the hotel's roof also makes it accessible from the air.

Designed by the international architecture firm of WS Atkins & Partners Overseas and completed in 2002, the Burj Al Arab is unique in terms of both its structure and the innovative technologies that were employed for its construction.

176 and 176-177 This ultra-luxurious hotel in the typical shape of a billowing sail was built in front of the Dubai waterfront on an artificial islet connected to the mainland by way of a 919-ft (280-m) long bridge. Its form recaptures that of a sailing ship docked off the city's coast.

178 In these images, you can admire the detail of the lower part of the hotel's load-bearing frame where three arched structural ribs link to the pinnacle that is the highest point of the structure.

179 Near the highest point of the hotel, a circular platform was installed as a landing pad for visitors' helicopters and may be equipped for sports and promotional events as needed.

The hotel belongs to the Jumeirah Group, headed by Dubai's ruler Sheikh Mohammed, which also owns many other luxury hotels in Dubai (including the Jumeirah Beach Hotel and the Emirates Tower) as well as in London and New York.

The Burj Al Arab has 202 suites all overlooking the sea and arranged on one or two levels, which vary in area from 1,830 to 8,395 sq ft (170–780 sq m). All the rooms are luxurious and boast all the latest technological amenities. The hotel has three restaurants – including an underwater one and another on the top floor with breathtaking views over the Gulf – lush gardens, huge swimming pools, an exceptionally well-equipped wellness center, a boutique, and everything necessary to ensure that its guests' stays are as comfortable as possible. The opulence of the interiors, with gleaming Italian marble, glistening walls covered with 22-carat gold leaf, richly decorated precious carpets, gilded ceilings, discreet downlighting, traditional wall decorations, and a 597-ft (180-m) high atrium combine to create an exclusive fairytale atmosphere, like something out of the

Arabian Nights. The Burj Al Arab's boat-inspired architecture, resembling as it does a wind-filled sail, a billowing spinnaker, is intended to establish a symbolic link with Dubai's seafaring origins. In order to build the hotel it was necessary to use a steel frame resting on piles driven 120 ft (36 m) into the seabed.

The frame consists of three large white masts, two of which curve to form an arch, rising from the corners of a triangular plan and meeting at the top. There are joined together by horizontal beams further strengthened by diagonal trusses. The structural skeleton was subsequently completed with a double membrane specifically developed to regulate solar radiation and to allow diffused lighting of the interiors. This sail is coated with Teflon, a polymer able to withstand extremely high temperatures.

The Burj Al Arab's sculptural form and technological image are enhanced at night by a light show that transforms the huge luminous sail into a sort of iridescent colored lighthouse.   O.E.B.

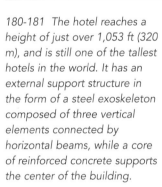

180-181 The hotel reaches a height of just over 1,053 ft (320 m), and is still one of the tallest hotels in the world. It has an external support structure in the form of a steel exoskeleton composed of three vertical elements connected by horizontal beams, while a core of reinforced concrete supports the center of the building.

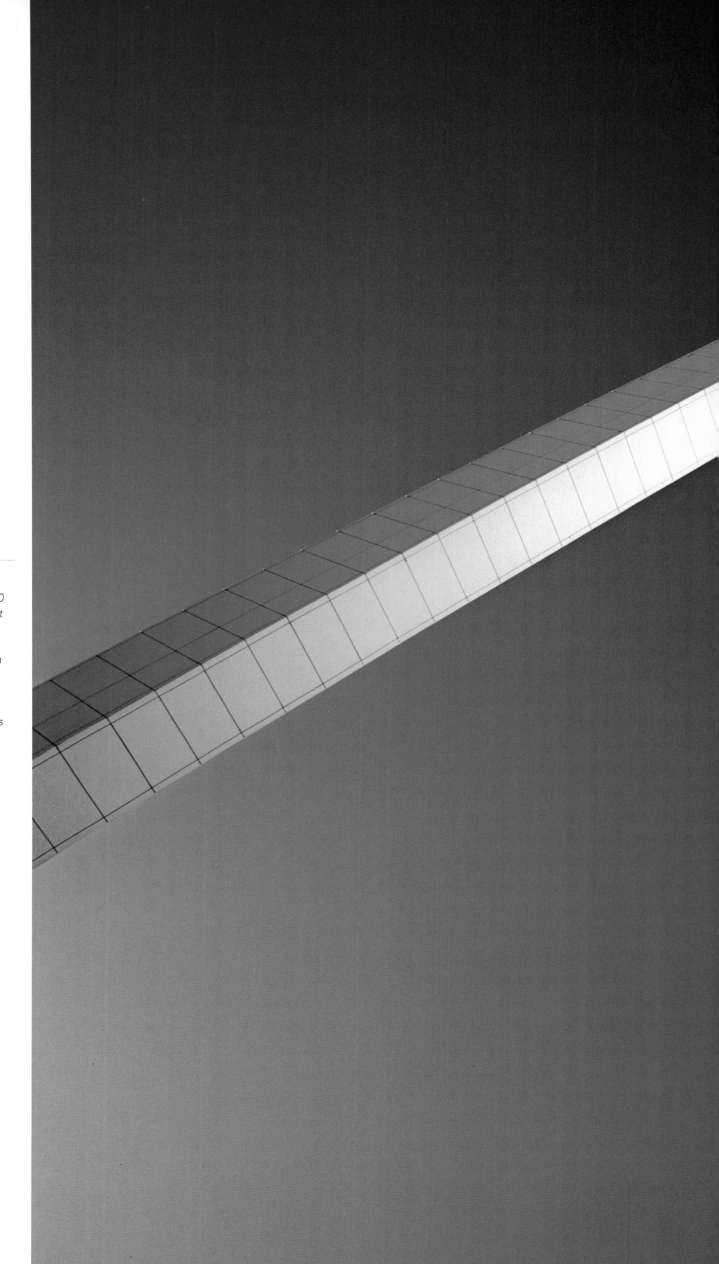

182-183 On the side of the building, the support structure was left exposed with its arched ribs, horizontal beams, and bracing girders, behind which the network of modular buffer panels are visible.

183 The building's sail effect was achieved through the use of teflon, a special fabric based on glass fiber, which has good thermal inertia and therefore resists high temperatures very well.

184 The Burj Al Arab has numerous restaurants connected to other parts of the structure through tunnels constructed in various materials, finishes, and colors. Among these is a very original underwater restaurant, the Al Mahara Seafood Restaurant, accessible only by means of a small submarine that leaves from the hotel lobby.

185 The entrance hall area is one of the most original and distinctive parts of this remarkable building. In addition to the beautiful decorative multicolored flooring, the ceilings are also sculpted. There is also a delightful waterfall that contributes to perfecting the overall atmosphere of tranquillity and luxurious escapism.

186-187 Gurgling fountains and other water features, tapered columns finished in gilt stucco, and blue ceilings suggesting starry skies are some of the interior details designed by Khuan Chew, architect for the Sultan of Brunei's palace, the Dubai international airport, and Jumeirah vacation resorts.

187 The central part of the hotel contains a large open space of 54 floors onto which all of the suites look. It is among the tallest hotels in the world of its type, defined by a system of tapered pseudo-columns that create a gigantic order, creating a decorative and magnificent display that recaptures the classical eras of Islamic architecture.

188-189 The large central atrium onto which the suite corridors face reflects light hitting its teflon wall, which is an innovative material that allows the passage of diffused light and thermally insulates the interior spaces.

190-191 This photorealistic illustration shows the horizontal plane that comprises the whole development and the jetties, ramps, and piers springing up around the tourist marina. In this image, the dense vegetation that surrounds and shades the building is particularly evident.

190 bottom The floor plan indicates the dialectic relationship that the building complex has with its surroundings. This is an intentionally artificial initiative that sharply interrupts the coastline, creating a protected inlet that is not only popular with the hotel guests but is also attracting a local crowd to its shops and coffee bars.

W Hotel

DUBAI

The W Hotel Dubai will be located in the heart of Marsa al Khor, the Festival City, and will be the largest and most prestigious hotel in the area. It has been designed by the famous French architect Jean Nouvel and will have 250 sumptuous rooms and 100 suites, a spa, several restaurants, swimming pools, nightclubs, boutiques, and all the other facilities that make an establishment of this kind comfortable and luxurious. Unlike many other Dubai hotels, the W Hotel will not be a tall building, rather it will be laid out horizontally over an area of approximately 560,000 sq ft (52,000 sq m). Its estimated cost has been put at over 100 million U.S. dollars.

The most distinctive feature of the hotel's design is that it makes a clean break with the curved forms of the buildings of the surrounding urban landscape. It will constitute a very evident interruption on the waterfront, projecting over 300 ft (90 m) into the Persian Gulf and forming an intentionally artificial inlet, which will be used as a marina for large and small boats. In this basin the land will engage with the water through a series of horizontal planes and overlapping wooden platforms arranged in different directions and on different levels, from the quays along the promenade to the building's flat roof.

ATELIERS JEAN NOUVEL

191 This architectural design may be interpreted as a metaphor for a large ship docked on the coast, where wooden platforms, conceived as the natural extension of Dubai's Corniche promenade, symbolize the jetty and the ship's main deck. In addition to promoting a direct relationship with the water, the hotel's "C" form creates an artificial bay where yachts can dock, protected from the heat and wind. Its Parisian architect also introduced a large green wall that acts as a vertical extension of the nearby park.

192-193 This plan shows the proposed design of a building without any interruption to the continuity between the interior and exterior in order to establish a direct visual relationship between the sunny wharves and the comfortable spaces of the hall.

192 bottom The thick vegetation shades the exterior and moderates the effects of the desert wind, and also becomes an integral part of the façades where rooms also include private balconies.

193 Dazzling plays of light and reflection enrich the interiors and other spaces, giving you the impression of being in an almost magical and fantastical environment.

Its set-back position will allow the W Hotel to have an impact on the area and will make it immediately distinguishable from the rest of the urban fabric. The complex will be built on a courtyard plan, which opens onto the Gulf, and will be developed around the small artificial basin that is an extension of the Corniche promenade. This will be the site of the main outdoor activities, with a public promenade, bars, restaurants, and jetties with berths for luxury motor yachts. The hotel's main wing will be raised on *pilotis*, projecting over the waters of the Gulf, ending in a quay, perpendicular to the coast, where large vessels will be able to dock. Smaller boats will be able to moor in the innermost part of the harbor, accessed by passing under a pedestrian bridge. The basement of the building will house a parking lot for guests. Particular care and attention have been dedicated to the design of the interiors, which will be characterized by an elegant minimalist style far removed from the extravagance of other luxury hotels throughout Dubai.

The figurative language of the project is based on metaphors associated with the nautical world. Objects and forms inspired by hulls, sails, and keels can be discerned in the profile of the hotel, its roof, rooms, and decorative motifs. Everything is characterized by elegant luxury, both the exteriors and the interiors, which have been designed to merge seamlessly. The complex will resemble a luxurious cruise ship, with decks overlooking the sea, leisure areas, cabins and even sails, and will be embellished by lush vegetation that has left the surrounding gardens to invade the imaginary vessel.

194 top and 194-195 top Hotel guests observing such a well-designed green space from their rooms may have the illusion of being in a lush forest rather than on the arid coast of Dubai.

194-195 bottom In suites embellished by materials such as wood and glass, both natural and artificial lighting play a fundamental role while being modified by elements providing shade.

Environmental comfort and the regulation of temperature and humidity inside the building will also be fundamental features, and have determined the architect's principal technological choices and also some of the structural solutions. A sophisticated system of mechanical blinds and brises-soleils will regulate solar radiation on the façades and in the rooms, controlling the amount of light and air allowed to enter the rooms at various times of day. The rooms will be set back from the façade in order to create loggias that will act as a buffer area, providing both insulation from the heat and privacy, and separating the inside from the outside and offering further spaces from which the sea views may be enjoyed. On the opposite side thick vegetation will shade the otherwise sunny outer façades and – together with the sea breezes – moderate the effects of the humid winds from the desert. The same effect will be achieved by the asymmetric sail membranes that will shade the roof.   O.E.B.

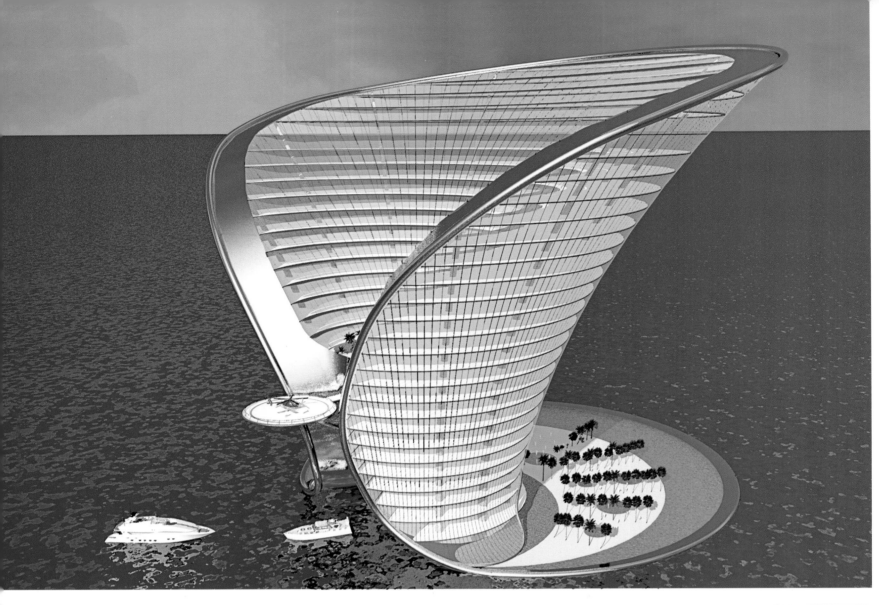

Apeiron Island Hotel

DUBAI

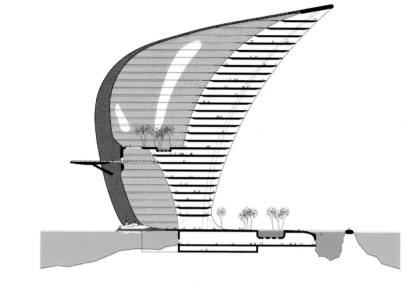

Despite the simple circular form of its plan, the Apeiron Hotel is undoubtedly one of the most bizarre buildings ever conceived. Indeed, the futuristic project designed by London-based Sybarite Architects features an amazing seven-star hotel (one of two in Dubai, the other is the Burj Al Arab) to be built over a quarter of a mile off the coast in the Persian Gulf. The unique design of this 607-ft (185-m) tall building resembles the silhouette of a sea anemone. It will be accessible only by sea or by air and will feature berths for large yachts and a suspended helipad. It is destined to become a new icon of Arabian architecture.

The name Apeiron comes from the cosmological theory developed by the pre-Socratic Greek philosopher Anaximander (c.610 B.C.–c.546 B.C.), who postulated that the infinite (*apeiron*) was the source and end of all things. *Apeiron* therefore denotes an indefinite, vague, and incommensurable source, from which the universe is derived and into which everything dissolves. Consequently, it can be equated with the concepts of the unknowable and infinity. This allows us to understand the concept underlying the formal and figurative aspects of the building, which, despite its indeterminate appearance, has a plan recalling the diagram that the Greek philosopher engraved on a tablet, and is conceived like an object that emerges from the water in a sort of cosmic embrace, or a funnel that captures and circulates the sea breeze and the vibrations of the universe.

The Apeiron will stand on a 285,000-sq-ft (26,480-sq-m) artificial island equipped with a beach, pools at various temperatures and with different lighting effects at night, and even a lagoon with a sculpted seafloor featuring corals and reef plants.

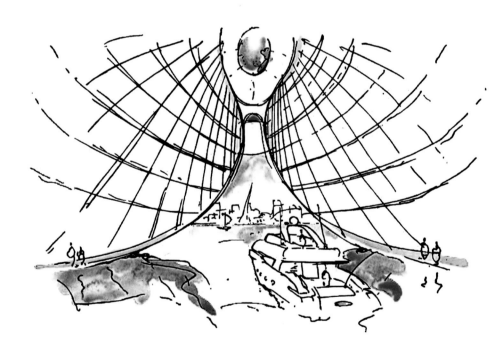

196 *This small artificial circular island is made up of disk shapes with tapered strips that create crescent images. The first circular shape takes form in the exterior promenade that narrows to a reflective strip framing the hotel, making up the perimeter of the entire complex. The second is an artificial circle of water that becomes the Crescent Lagoon. The third is a disk-shaped sandy* area that constitutes a private beach, and the fourth is a garden containing the last circular shape that fades as it rises towards the sky.

197 top *This section shows how a part of the complex was developed below sea level.*

197 center and bottom *Design sketches demonstrate access points to the hotel.*

The building will have a total area of approximately 3 million sq ft (279,000 sq m), with 28 horseshoe-shaped floors that increase in size the higher the floor.

Two underground floors will house an art gallery, a gym, a wellness center, a bar, and a restaurant, all with underwater views, as well as the service and maintenance rooms. In addition to a jetty for yachts at the core of the complex, the ground floor will boast a lobby with a 164-ft (50-m) high atrium, boutiques, and access to the beach, complete with palm trees and a panoramic promenade around the

perimeter of the island. The upper floors will have a cinema, conference rooms, bars, restaurants, and 438 sumptuous luxury suites of various sizes, ranging from 1,938 to 8,073 sq ft (180–750 sq m), served by a staggering 14 elevators plus 8 service elevators. An artificial jungle inhabited by butterflies and other tropical insects is planned for the top two floors. The different zones of the complex, such as the outer garden on the 11th floor that will greet guests arriving by helicopter, will be characterized by spectacular lighting effects and reflections of sky and water.

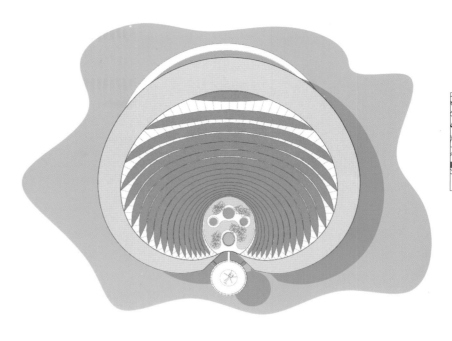

198-199 Access to the hotel is guaranteed by a heliport suspended at the ninth floor and by a private boat dock hollowed out from the central part of the building, where a private, protected marina is directly connected to the entrance atrium.

199 top This plan shows the development of the various levels and highlights the general forms that describe the exterior spaces.

199 center From both a second-level bar and boutique, guests can look at the beach and the sea lagoon, and watch boats that are docking.

199 bottom A suspended garden on the 11th level decorates the space with freshwater tanks of exotic plant life. These tanks allow light to filter through to the restaurant and art gallery below.

The structure will be built from steel and reinforced concrete. Its internal façade will feature louvers to regulate solar radiation, while the external one, composed prevalently of transparent windows, will enjoy the shade created by the profile of the building. A reflective ribbon frame covered with silvered glass tiles will blur the separation between the sea and the sky, making the Apeiron merge with the natural elements. Part of the building will be covered with solar cells that will provide two-thirds of its energy requirements. O.E.B.

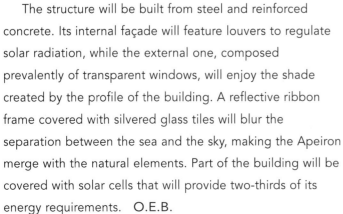

ETA Hotel

DUBAI

The design of the ETA Hotel demonstrates that even among the glittering forest of skyscrapers that currently forms Dubai's skyline, the product of the city's endless quest for the exceptional and extraordinary, there is room for smaller buildings with a less assertive visual impact. This hotel, designed by the Indian firm of Sanjay Puri & Nimish Shah, is aimed at businesspeople, occasional tourists, and short-stay visitors. It will have 68 rooms, a restaurant, a bar, a health club, a swimming pool on the roof, and two underground floors for parking.

The planned building will have a floor area of approximately 800,000 sq ft (74,300 sq m) and will be located in a high-density commercial area of the city. Both sides of the street on which it will stand are lined with relatively small buildings, of similar size to the hotel. In order to overcome the anonymous nature of the district and to distinguish the building from its immediate surroundings, the architects devised a structure that is somewhat similar to a huge stone monolith rather than to traditional forms of hotel architecture. It is formed by an intersecting series of non-orthogonal surfaces, which create a skin composed of an undefined number of trapezoidal planes, creating a faceted solid. From a distance it will resemble a sort of iceberg floating on a sea of nondescript buildings. This form will give the hotel an extremely distinctive appearance, rejecting all associations or links with its urban context.

200-201 and 201 bottom
This building fits into the urban checkerboard by reappropriating the proportions of surrounding buildings, but it completely diverges from them through its original form that refers to an exacting and unified architecture *achieved through very minimal spacing and an enclosure constructed of concrete. The resulting building is strongly self-referential and does not seem to dialogue with any of the other components within its context.*

202 During the design phase, Sanjay Puri Architects assert that they had to manage the visual results of their experimental architecture, with particular emphasis given to artificial lighting.

202-203 This detail of the building's foundations shows the entrance area and glass enclosure system in the corners. This architectural solution was utilized to distinguish the building's base by lightening the lower corner supports thereby obtaining a better concrete façade "envelope" effect.

The hard and introverted image of the design will be further accentuated by the reinforced concrete used for both the building's structural frame and its skin. This concrete skin will be punctuated by a series of small geometric openings derived from an Islamic motif, and will be repeated on the building's many façades. This will create a pattern of solids and voids reminiscent of the grille of the *burqa* (a traditional woman's garment worn in several Islamic countries) and will filter the view of the city enjoyed by the hotel's guests.

The openings will allow diffused light to enter the rooms, filtered through a loggia that will create a protected space between the interior and the exterior of the building. This expedient will produce a sort of cavity protecting the rooms from the humid heat of the city. At the same time it will significantly improve the efficiency of the artificial air-conditioning system and increase the privacy of the rooms from the occupants of the nearby buildings. The 20-ft (6-m) high atrium will also accentuate the building's irregular design, echoing the angles and trapezoidal forms of the exterior in the large windows that will illuminate the ground-floor lobby. O.E.B.

tadao ando architects and as

partners LLP *(guggenheim museum)* –

– zaha hadid & associates *(abu d*

(guggenheim pavilions)

culture

ociates *(maritime museum)* – gehry
eliers jean nouvel *(louvre abu dhabi)*
performing arts centre) – asymptote

SAADIYAT ISLAND

SAADIYAT ISLAND ("ISLAND OF HAPPINESS") IS A COLOSSAL CONSTRUCTION PROJECT THAT WILL CREATE A CULTURAL, RESIDENTIAL, COMMERCIAL, AND LEISURE COMPLEX ON AN ARID SANDY AREA LYING 600 YARDS (550 M) OFF THE COAST OF ABU DHABI ISLAND.

Sheikh Khalifa bin Zayed Al Nahyan aims to transform the rich capital of the emirate into a new Mecca of luxury tourism by focusing on art and culture to generate income. The principal aim is to allow the smooth transition of the local economy from its dependence on its fossil fuel resources to new forms of revenue, while updating the country's image, which is still closely associated with traditional values.

This extremely ambitious project involves some of the most prestigious names in international architecture. Skidmore, Owings and Merrill was commissioned to design the overall plan and the necessary road and transport infrastructure, while Gensler was invited to draw up the detailed plan for the entire island. The aim is to equip an area half the size of the island of Bermuda with 2 golf courses, 29 hotels (including a 7-star one) able to accommodate over 7,000 people, 3 marinas with 1,000 berths, 12 miles (19 km) of white sand beaches, more than 8,000 private villas and 38,000 apartments in complexes arranged like a "string of pearls," eventually allowing the island to house around 15,000 residents.

The key part of the project is undoubtedly the Cultural District, dedicated to art and culture, with museums, concert halls, art galleries, exhibition halls, and many other facilities. It is the first and most strategic stage in the urban and cultural development plan backed by the Tourism Development and Investment Company of Abu Dhabi (TDIC) and has coincided with the international presentation of the first four great projects that will constitute the economic powerhouse of the entire district. The new cultural center, scheduled to be completed by the end of 2018, is conveniently linked to the city and Abu Dhabi International Airport by two causeways, as well as a light railway able to transport the thousands of tourists who will flock to Saadiyat Island from all over the world to admire its architectural splendors and the important works of art that they will house.

The complex will feature a Louvre museum designed by Jean Nouvel and a Guggenheim museum by Frank Gehry, the Abu Dhabi Performing Arts Centre with five theaters designed by Zaha Hadid, and a Maritime Museum by Tadao Ando. In a sort of declaration of global cooperation, four international architects (an American, an Asian, a European, and a British-Iraqi) have agreed to pool their highly personal talents, backed by Arab petrodollars, to form a new alliance of Eastern and Western culture. They have thus joined forces to realize a futuristic project, with the utmost freedom of expression, whose dual focus is art and architecture, thus translating an age-old dream into reality.

The District of Arts is completed by the Sheikh Zayed National Museum, which is dedicated to Abu Dhabi's history and traditions, and consists of 19 pavilions where

an art biennale will be held. The complex has been designed by such famous architects as Greg Lynn, Hani Rashid of Asymptote, and the Beijing-based Studio Pei-Zhu. A mile-long navigable channel connects the pavilions. Long-term projects include the construction of a creative campus with fine arts schools destined to support and promote the artistic sensibility of the local population.   O.E.B.

206-207 Some of the most well-known designers were called upon to create architectural designs that would accommodate shows, concerts, and other events.

207 bottom This island has a triangular shape: to the west is the Persian Gulf and to the east a canal.

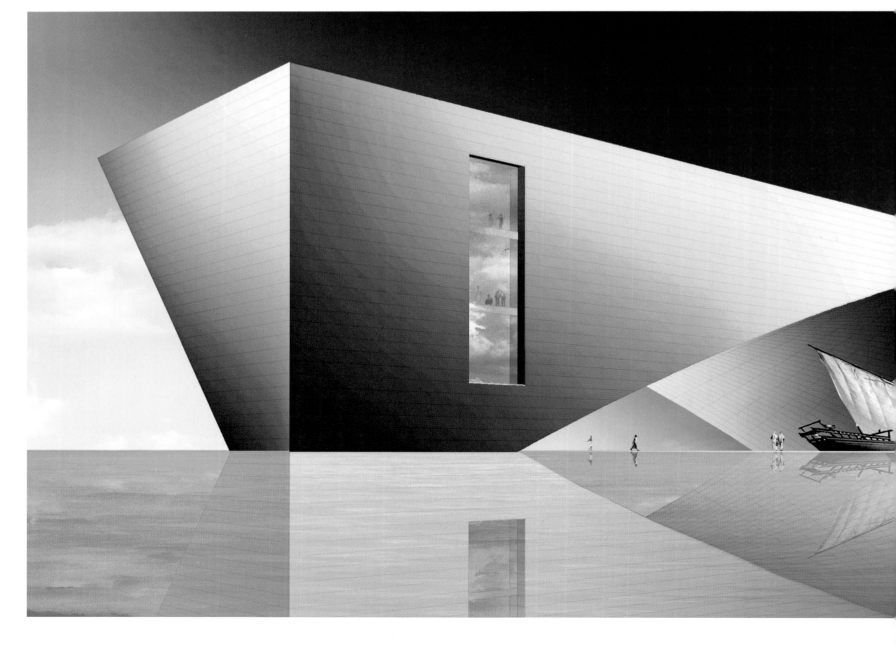

Maritime Museum
ABU DHABI

The Maritime Museum was designed by the renowned Japanese architect Tadao Ando. The design simultaneously engages with the inhospitable landscape of the immediate surroundings of Saadiyat Island, while seeking to identify with the city of Abu Dhabi's traditional links with the sea and the world of shipping. It is the symbolic representation of a space where water and land meet visually and physically in a sort of intimate embrace. Consequently, the as yet unbuilt museum's form will be clean and linear, carved out of a single volume without any decoration. Its distinguishing features will be an asymmetrical arch and a fissure created by an oblique line, which makes it resemble a cliff eroded by the wind and waves of the Persian Gulf. This will create an inner cavity, like a sinuous coastal recess, where the land is reflected in the water. Dhows, the traditional local sailboats that have transported men and cargoes over the Indian Ocean for centuries, will float in this interior space. A long gangway that seems suspended above the water will lead to the entrance of the museum, evocatively positioned beneath the waterline.

In addition to the entrance hall and reception area, the basement of the Maritime Museum will have an enormous aquarium, allowing visitors to admire many marine species in their natural habitat, and view the keel of a traditional dhow from various angles. The other floors will house the museum areas, the bookshop, a bar, a meeting room, and educational workshops. All the rooms are accessed by ramps, suspended walkways and floating bridges that will conduct visitors through an intense visual experience, enriched with sophisticated effects of natural light and shade.

The open space is defined by a regular grid that will not only determine the dimensions of the platform on which the museum will stand, but will also dictate the layout of the rows of trees that will mark the gradual transition for visitors from the bustling city to the ethereal tranquility of the museum. The building (354 ft/107 m long, 118 ft/36 m wide, and 89 ft/27 m tall) will be constructed entirely from bare concrete and will be completed by a long colonnade, also made from reinforced concrete. O.E.B.

208-209 top The large open space created within the structure's interior exposes the museum to its surrounding environment and emphasizes the presence of the waters. Visitors must travel over a walkway that seems suspended over the water to access the museum space below sea level.

208-209 bottom The concrete envelope that contains the entire building is interrupted only by the clean lines of a window, which enables the visitors to the exposition halls and spaces on the three levels above sea level to have views looking out over the waters of the strait.

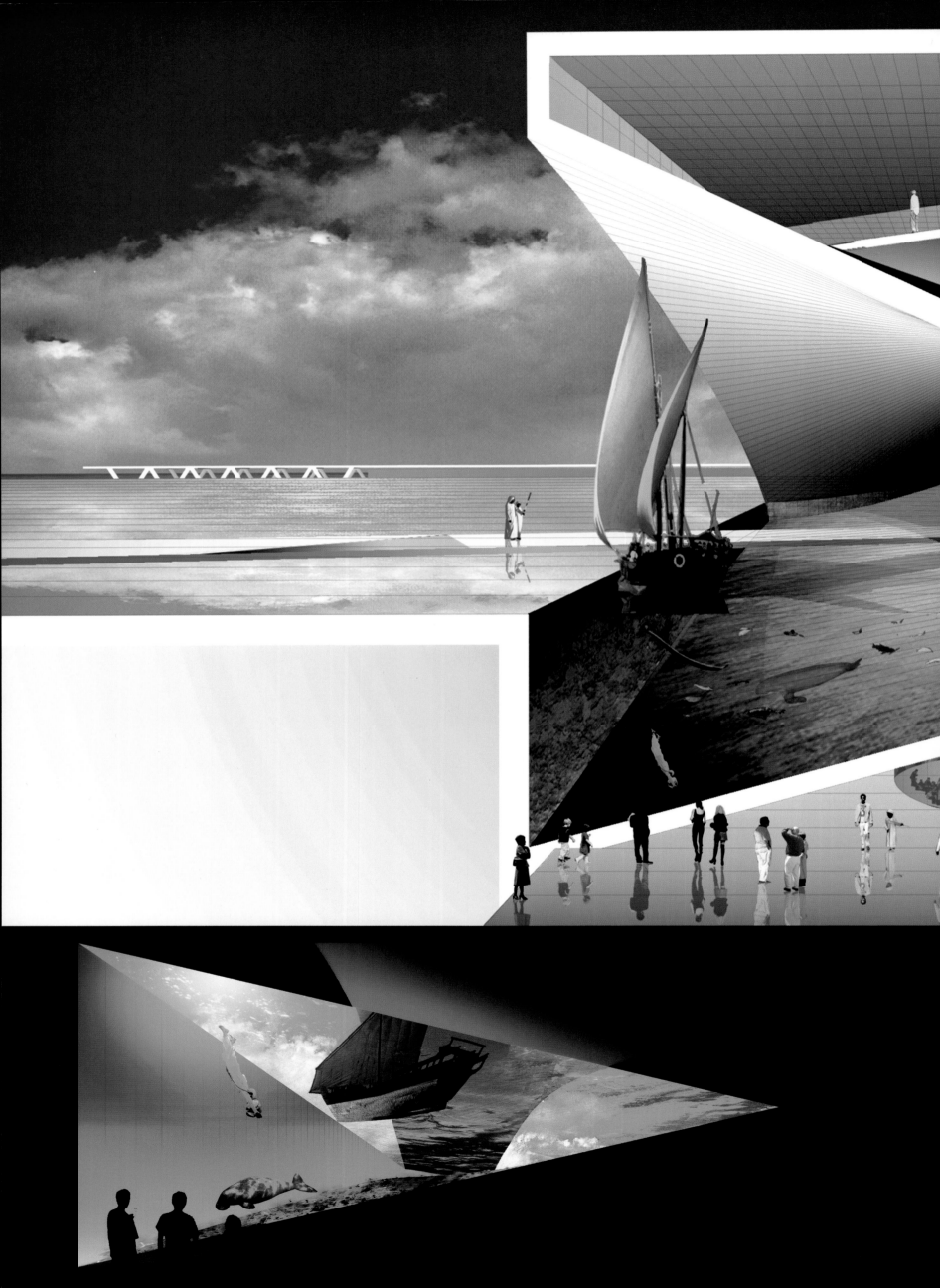

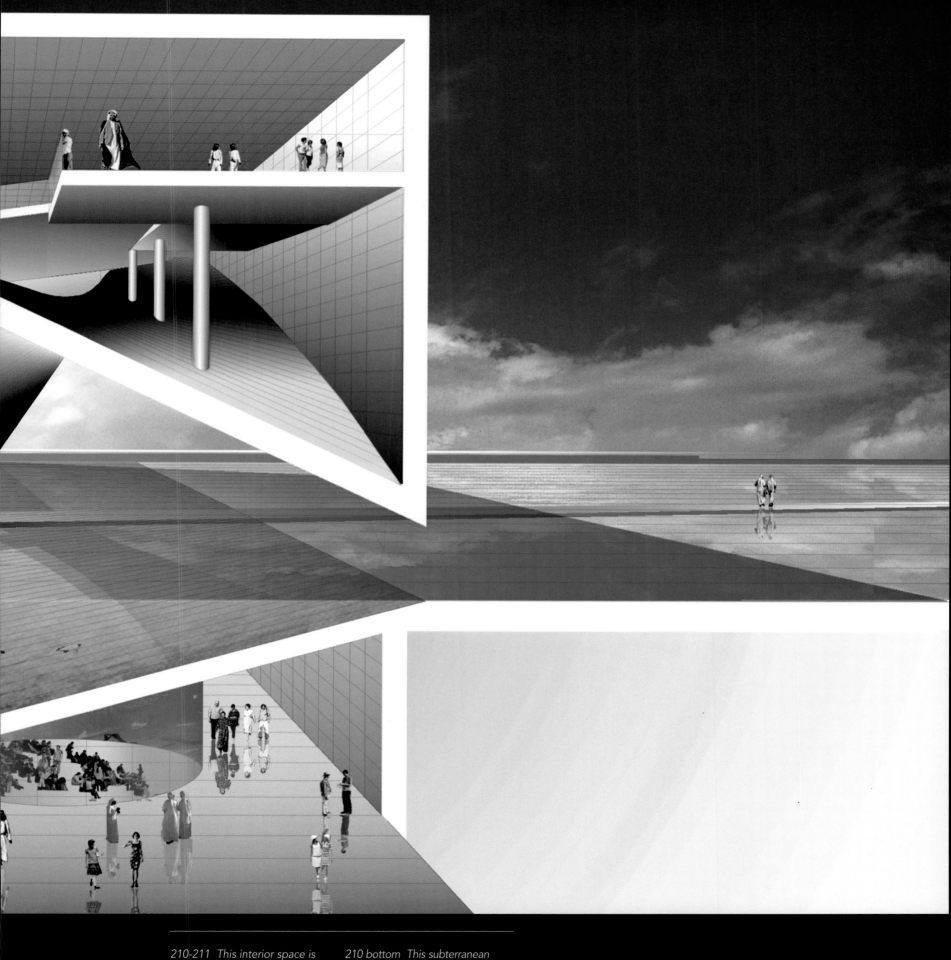

210-211 This interior space is similar to the hold of a large ship where suspended gangways and guided routes lead visitors to discover the secrets of the sea through various exhibition museum spaces.

210 bottom This subterranean space accommodates an enormous aquarium where a dhow floats on the water's surface with sails unfurled. From this viewpoint, visitors may watch the fauna and flora along the coral reef.

Guggenheim Museum

ABU DHABI

Following the establishment of museums in New York, Venice, Berlin, Bilbao, and Las Vegas, a sixth Guggenheim Museum is planned in the United Arab Emirates, on the natural island of Saadiyat off the coast of Abu Dhabi. Designed by the famous American architect Frank Gehry, who also designed the Bilbao museum, it is the largest of all the museums belonging to the Solomon R. Guggenheim Foundation.

In Abu Dhabi, Gehry has designed an array of spectacular sculptural forms. The vaguely futuristic-looking mega-project is reminiscent of a cubist painting. Cones up to 265 ft (80 m) tall seem to rest on enormous parallelepipeds, while their height, form, and design all underscore the structure's multiple functional components. In his quest for dynamism, Gehry has drawn on elements of the local architectural tradition, such as wind towers and Bedouin tents. Several of the technological solutions employed in the design are also derived from local construction techniques, such as the conical galleries that channel air into the interiors, cooling the rooms. The outer walls are built from many different colors and types of stone, further emphasizing the different exhibition halls. The Abu Dhabi museum will be set among greenery, surrounded by golf courses and luxury hotels, and will accommodate up to 150,000 visitors.

212 This museum, designed by Gehry, is located at a unique site at one end of Saadiyat Island. The resulting structure is the only one that reflects the culture of this district by looking directly onto the open sea, while other museums face their urban environments.

212-213 top Among other things, this impressive building will accommodate the Abu Dhabi Biennial of Art, which will be housed inside two large galleries. The museum is intended to promote a love of art and culture throughout the United Arab Emirates.

212-213 bottom The establishment of the Emirates branch of the Guggenheim Museum is proposed for a site near the mouth of the navigable canal intended for the Guggenheim Pavilions, which have designed by the New York firm, Asymptote.

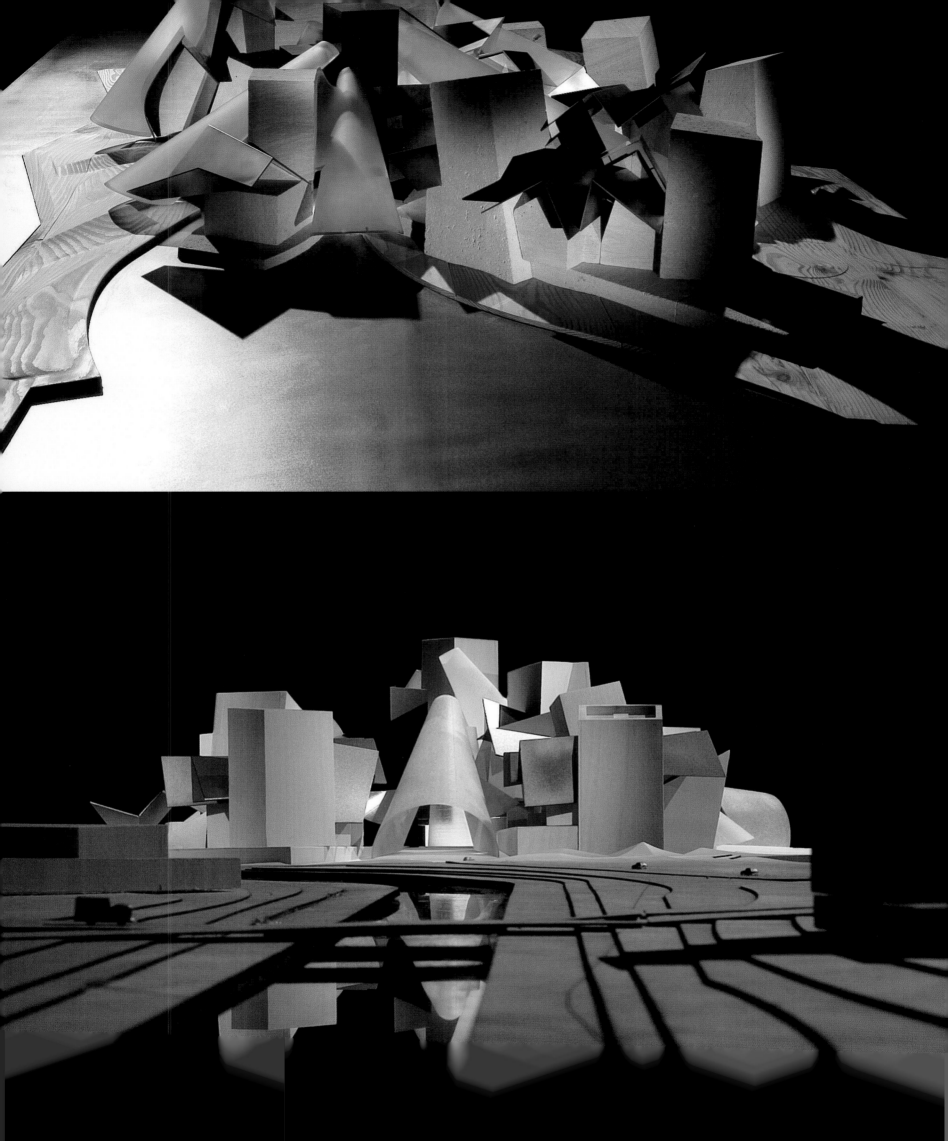

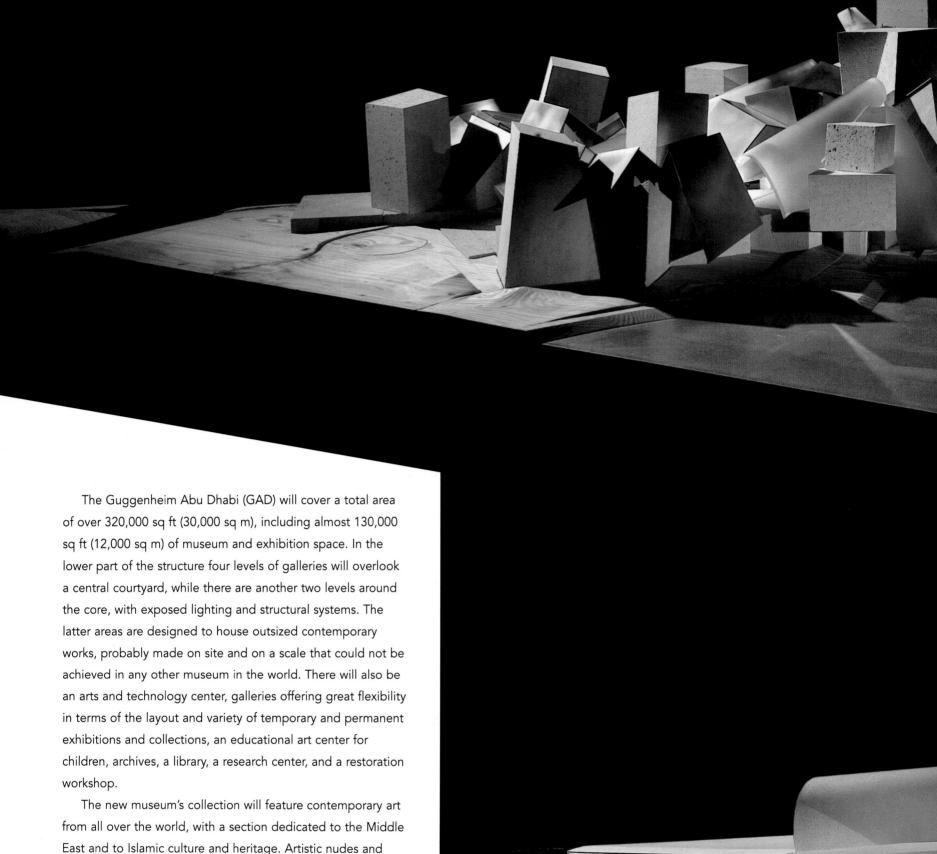

The Guggenheim Abu Dhabi (GAD) will cover a total area of over 320,000 sq ft (30,000 sq m), including almost 130,000 sq ft (12,000 sq m) of museum and exhibition space. In the lower part of the structure four levels of galleries will overlook a central courtyard, while there are another two levels around the core, with exposed lighting and structural systems. The latter areas are designed to house outsized contemporary works, probably made on site and on a scale that could not be achieved in any other museum in the world. There will also be an arts and technology center, galleries offering great flexibility in terms of the layout and variety of temporary and permanent exhibitions and collections, an educational art center for children, archives, a library, a research center, and a restoration workshop.

The new museum's collection will feature contemporary art from all over the world, with a section dedicated to the Middle East and to Islamic culture and heritage. Artistic nudes and religious figures or themes that are not consistent with Islamic morality are absent.   O.E.B.

214-215 The Abu Dhabi Guggenheim has all of the visual and compositional characteristics that made the celebrated American architect famous, even when the impressive classical spatial volumes, sculpted forms, distorted planes, broken lines, and variety of colors in his free-thinking architecture are reinterpreted in local cultural terms and according to the requests, indications, and expectations of his client in this country.

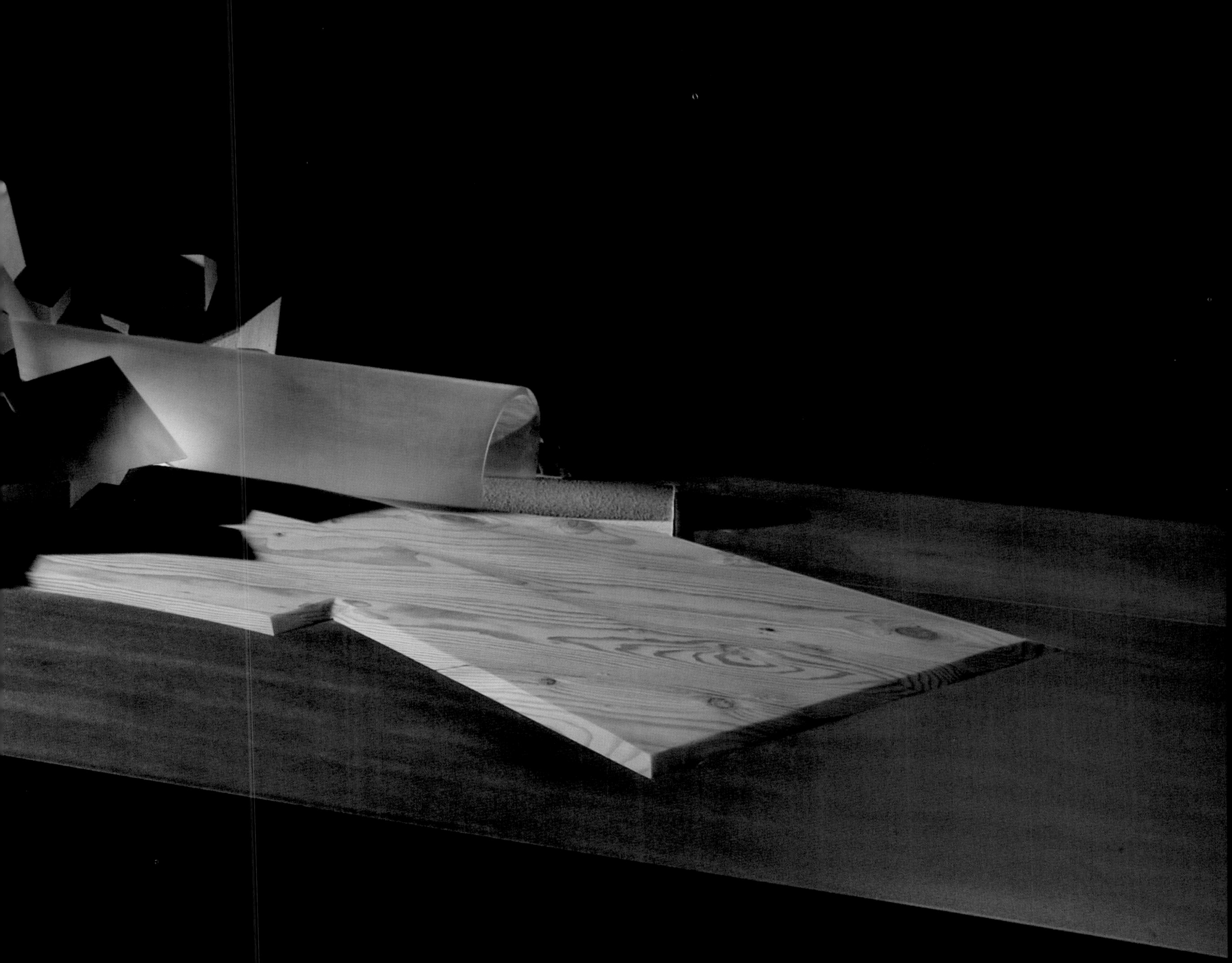

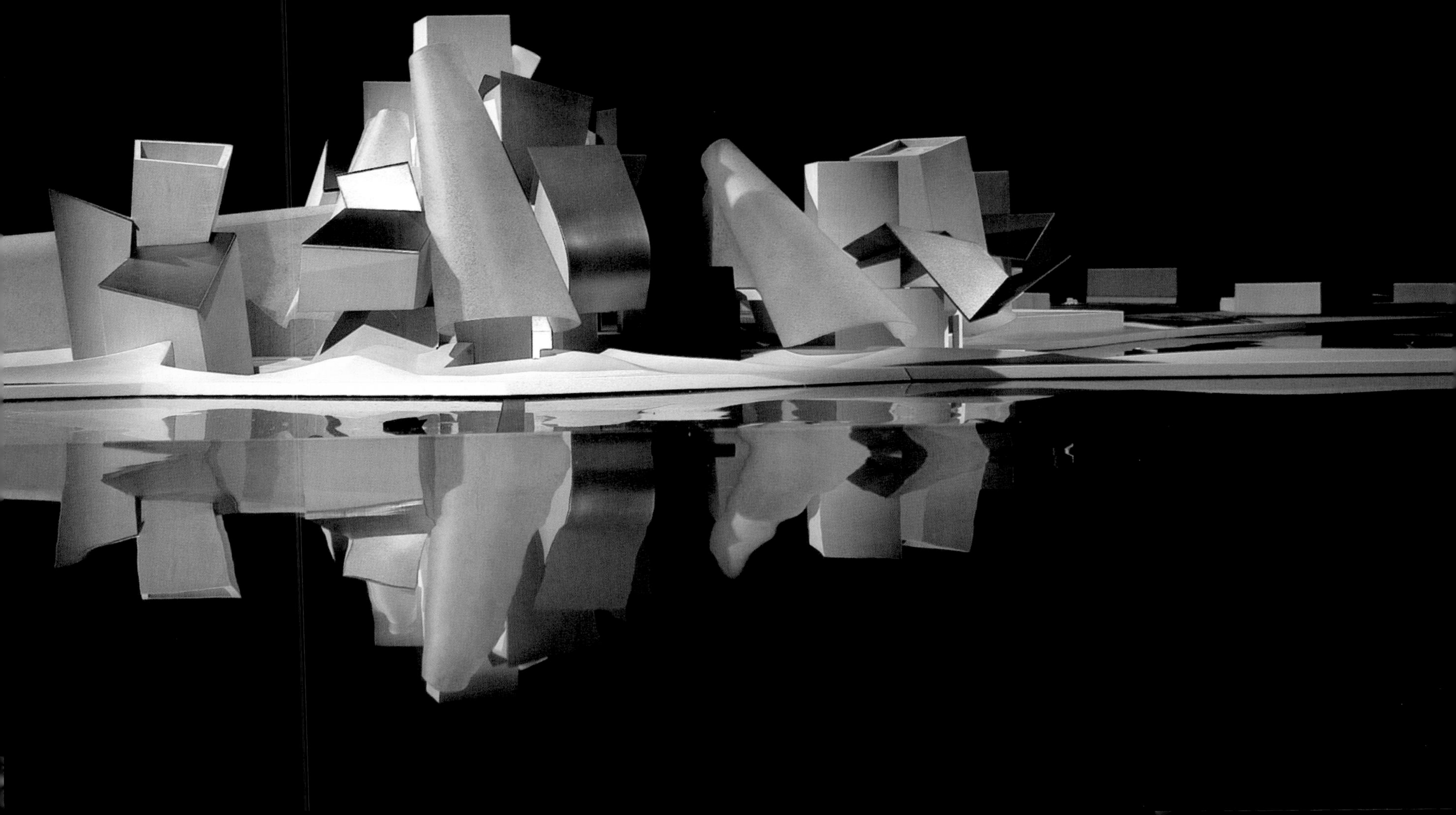

Louvre Abu Dhabi

ABU DHABI

Shortly after Jean Nouvel had been commissioned to design the Classical Museum, an international press conference was called to announce that it would be the first Louvre museum to be built outside France. Indeed, Abu Dhabi has signed a multi-million dollar agreement with the Louvre that means many of the museum's collections and works of art will be loaned to the city. The result is a sort of fantasy city that has detached itself from the desert in favor of the waters of the Persian Gulf; an unearthly microcosm built partly on the sand and partly beneath the sea.

The design of this complex building is comprised of many different spaces in the form of simple parallelepipeds, which will house the galleries, workshops, storerooms, bookshops, and service areas. However, the most distinctive element of

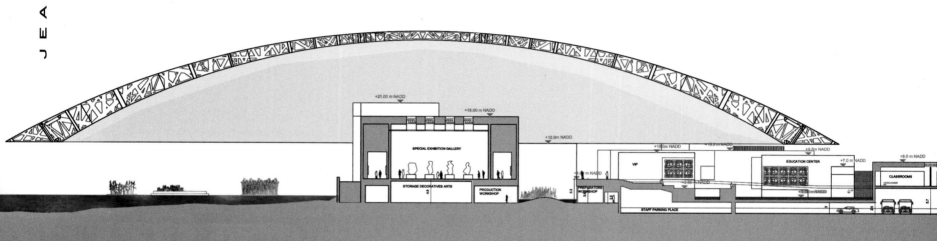

the design is its dome, an archetypal shape shared by all civilizations, which Nouvel has interpreted in an almost dream-like manner. The dome only partly covers the pavilions below and is formed by a mesh structure that supports and tautens a translucent, perforated photosensitive skin through which the natural light will be strikingly filtered, creating an ideal microclimate. Nouvel had already proposed a similar architectural membrane for the Dubai Opera House, but in this setting it appears more compelling and effective, as it is capable of evoking the otherworld quality of an unearthly, almost lunar, landscape.

The museum's design is inspired by the surrounding natural environment, and offers an architectural interpretation of the contrast between the arid land and the sea. Water is a fundamental element in the design. It will not only contribute to maintaining an ideal level of environmental comfort in the interiors, but will also create evocative glints and magical plays of light that will intertwine and merge with the rays of light filtering through the holes in the roof. The entire building has been intentionally designed as an elegant tribute to Islamic architecture.

In order to ensure the quality of the project, it will be overseen by the French Museums Agency, which represents prominent cultural institutions, including the Musée d'Orsay, the Pompidou Centre, the Guimet Museum, the Palace of Versailles, and the Louvre itself.   O.E.B.

216-217 top The cross section clarifies the design's proportions. The building occupies 258,333 sq ft (24,000 sq m), 86,111 (8,000) of which are designated for exhibition spaces. The cupola has a diameter of just over 590 ft (180 m) and a height of around 82 ft (25 m), distributing its weight over five load-bearing supports.

216-217 bottom The cupola is an archetypal form common to all people. It may take on diverse meanings, from a more dignified significance to a celebratory one or even simply assume a functional role, evoking the large tents of the Bedouin.

218-219 This museum is a small fantasy city built over the water and consists of white spatial volumes. In design, water and light play a crucial role after the best traditions of great Arab architecture.

219 The spectacular cupola is the defining element in this design. It controls the amount of light that filters inside and facilitates the creation of an ideal interior microclimate. In the aerial view, it looks like lace through which you can catch a glimpse of the underlying geometric spaces that seem to float on water.

220-221 and 220 bottom
The shaded spaces of the
grand dome take on a surreal
appearance as light filtering
through the elaborate enclosure
and reflecting on the water
create an atmosphere of diffused
light yet simultaneously rich in
contrast.

Louvre Abu Dhabi

221 Water lapping at the steps and isolated pots of papyrus contribute to the layout of this exhibitional space, where the boundary between earth and water seems to disappear. Due primarily to nationalistic motivations, the question of lending its name to the Emirates museum generated a fierce debate in France. Nevertheless, the agreement was signed and it was not the first of its kind. In fact, Abu Dhabi can also boast the first branch of the Sorbonne, which opened in 2006.

Abu Dhabi Performing Arts Centre
ABU DHABI

The Abu Dhabi Performing Arts Center has been designed by British-Iraqi architect Zaha Hadid for the Solomon R. Guggenheim Foundation and the Tourism Development and Investment Company of Abu Dhabi (TDIC). The design is distinguished by its bizarre futuristic form that will make the building immediately recognizable among the other buildings on Saadiyat Island. The complex will house a drama academy and four theaters for shows, concerts, and operas, as well as a flexible auditorium with a maximum seating capacity of 6,300.

The design concept is the result of in-depth studies on the development and growth of living organisms and the transposition into architecture of the rules governing the organization of certain biological systems. The structure of the arts center is an example of a design process based on diagrams. Thus the architectural design is modeled on algorithms and energy flows, but also incorporates elements based on branches, legs, fruits, and foliage, reinforcing the organic metaphor.

The building's formal language is derived from the intersecting paths in Abu Dhabi's Cultural District, with particular emphasis on the pedestrian corridor that extends from the Sheikh Zayed National Museum to the central axis of the district before linking with the promenade. The resulting structure will be 203 ft (62 m) tall and 443 ft (135 m) wide, with 14 floors, including four below ground level. It

222 top As is the case with other British–Iraqi designs, the architectural forms in this plan seem to sprout from the ground and stretch out towards the sea as if they were living beings.

222-223 These interior spaces capture light through the spectacular glass windows that make up the façades, which have been designed starting from the formal logic inspired by nature and half-reveal a vein pattern similar to that found in leaves.

223 top The body of this building stretches dynamically towards the water, taking on the appearance of a marine creature ready to plunge into the sea. Its only bond with the land seems to be the access road at the rear of the building.

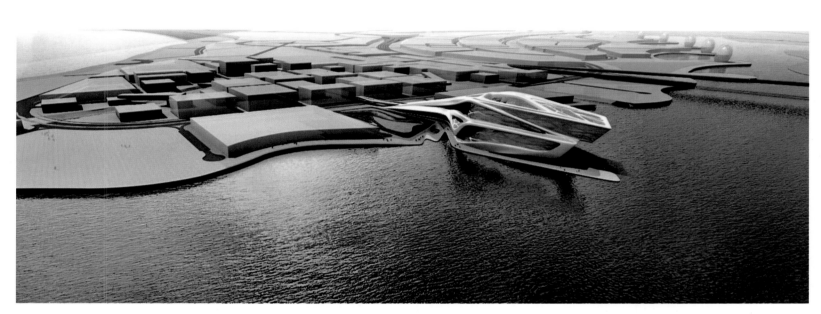

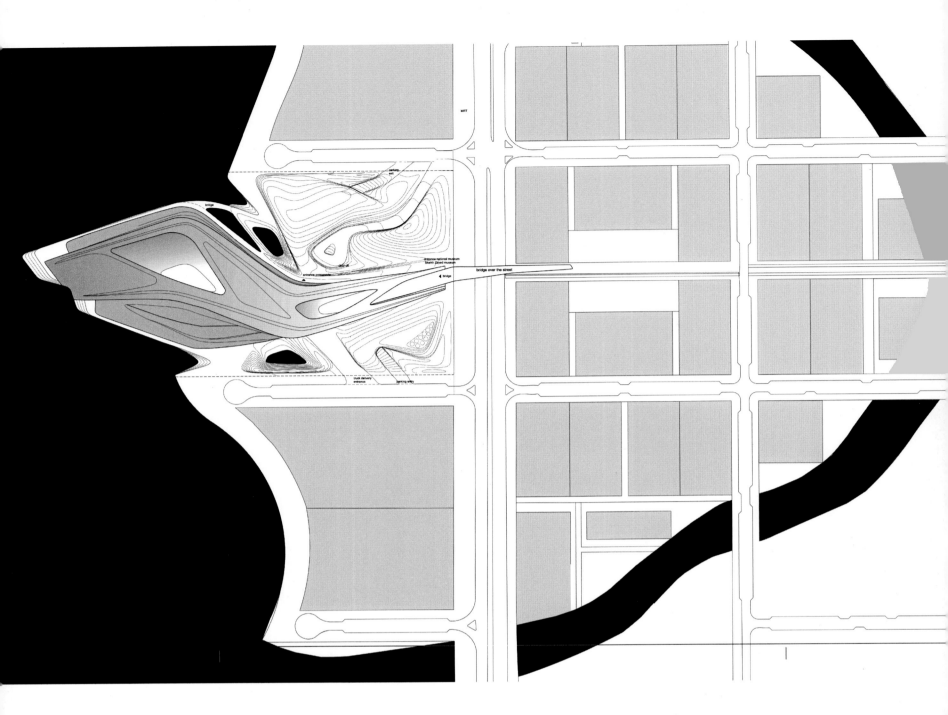

will be characterized by an elongated shape that projects towards the sea, whose sculptural form is influenced by the movement of the waves. The building will thus be a visual crescendo, culminating in an imposing and intricately structured organism. The five areas dedicated to events sprout like the buds of a climbing plant, unfolding in the quest for the concept of infinity represented by the sea.

The entrance to the building will be through the "tail" in its eastern section, which will incorporate the external pedestrian path, while the organism progressively grows towards the waters of the Gulf, generating an artificial web of intertwined branches. The concert hall will be above the four theaters. Its zenithal position will ensure splendid views over the city and abundant natural light. All the entrances to the theaters will face the sea. A large roof terrace will be connected to both the restaurant and the adjacent conference center. There will be several shops near the entrance, while the drama academy will be situated in the southern area above the experimental theater. O.E.B.

224 This work by Zaha Hadid breaks the rigid checkerboard of the urban fabric with fluid and sinuous forms that project towards the inlet that is home to the cultural buildings on Saadiyat Island. Its architectural form progressively grows, transforming into an organism that is increasingly complex and voluminous.

225 top Complex diagrams of molecular growth, mathematical models, and energy flow charts were transposed into this architecture, defining the support structure in this one-of-a-kind building.

225 center and bottom Sections that reach a height of 203 ft (62 m) show the interior organization, allowing us to understand the spatial complexity of its diverse functions. The top floor is illuminated by sunlight filtering from the zenith through a translucent enclosure.

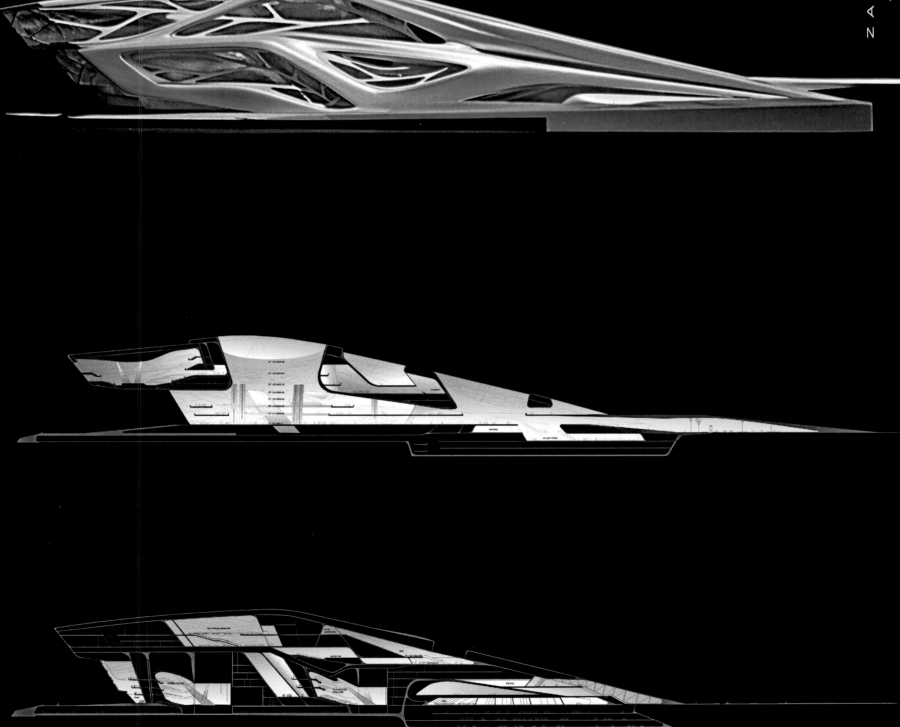

ZAHA HADID & ASSOCIATES

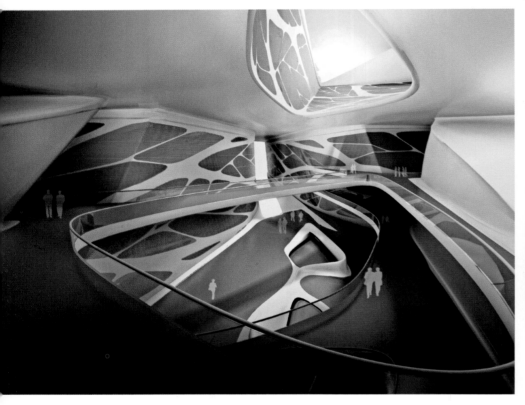

226 The planning of the interior space followed the same formal rules used for the exterior spaces. Dynamic, fluid areas accompany the visitor over the course of ramps, walkways, and winding uneven levels that open into the various rooms.

226-227 The large auditorium on the top level has a distinctly privileged position in the structure's interior. It has been design to allow visitors to enjoy incredible panoramic views to the horizon and with only the skies above them.

ASYMPTOTE

Guggenheim Pavilions
ABU DHABI

These two exhibition pavilions were designed by Hani Rashid and Lise Anne Couture, the principal architects and founding partners of the New York firm Asymptote Architecture. The pavilions will house two contemporary art galleries and other important collections, completing the extensive cultural facilities planned for Abu Dhabi's Saadiyat Island.

Unlike the other large-scale projects of the Cultural District, the Guggenheim Pavilions will not overlook the Persian Gulf, but instead will be situated in a more secluded position. As a result, they are not involved in the intense competition to produce the most outstanding building which appears to be raging between the architects working on the rest of the Saadiyat Island project. Instead, they will engage with each other, establishing a powerful intimate dialogue. Nevertheless, the structures are in no way inferior to the other cultural buildings in terms of formal innovation, architectural composition, and state-of-the-art construction techniques.

The two pavilions have a mysterious enigmatic shape. The largest building has five floors with a total area of 54,000 sq ft (5,000 sq m), while the smaller one has three floors with a total area of 27,000 sq ft (2,500 sq m). The two structures are linked by a sinuous bridge that will cross a mile-long navigable channel that empties into the sea. This bridge will emphasiz their connection not only on a formal, physical level but also in symbolic terms, because it is a clear reference to a sort of umbilical cord joining the two "bodies" into a single entity. The concept conveyed is of a filial relationship, as though one of the buildings has generated the other. The arrangement of the two structures appears influenced by the shapes and forms associated with the organic, such as insects

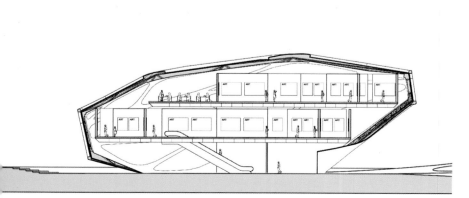

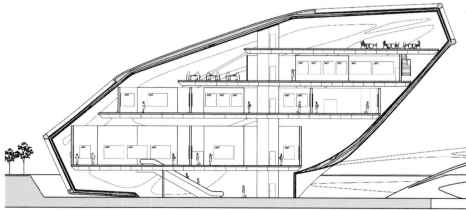

228-229 and 228 bottom The total surface area intended for shows and other cultural events is almost 80,730 sq ft (7,500 sq m), subdivided into two pavilions that are connected by a suspension bridge with a grid structure.

229 bottom The two pavilions have a special enclosure that fills the existing space between the structural ribs, and also a semipermeable membrane capable of regulating the flow of light into the interior.

230-231 In contrast to other
nearby structures intended for
promoting culture on Saadiyat
Island, Asymptote's building is
situated in the island's interior.
The two wings of the building
rise up on opposite sides of
a navigable canal.

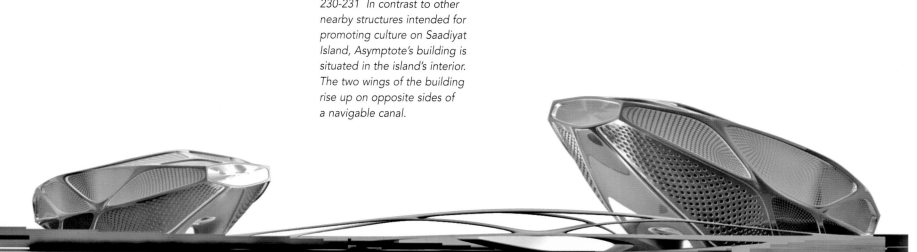

or seeds, as well as by references to the inorganic world, such as diamonds and precious stones set in the rock.

According to the architects, these pavilions with their functional, clearly defined, elegant design represent two ships, whose organic structural system conceals a high-tech shell. The upper part of this skin is perforated with openings that will filter the natural light and illuminate the interiors, creating a flexible dynamic space. Escalators will ensure easy access between the different levels.   O.E.B.

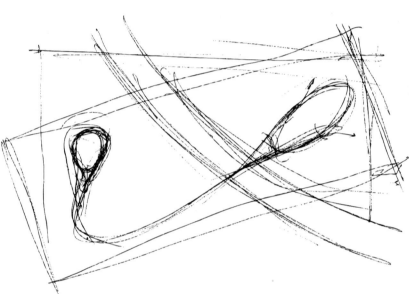

230 bottom and 231 bottom The form and structure of the two pavilions evoke an image of two objects linked both to the organic and inorganic worlds. Although the designers describe them as vessels, they are reminiscent of a couple of large amphibians that lie immobile, watching the flow of the water in the canal.

231 top The design is based on the theme of spatial experimentation in the digital age. They adopted a strategy of introducing an architecture that is experimental and forward-thinking, linked to themes of complexity and uncertainty, not static but tied to a constant fluidity adapted from the flow of information systems in the electronic age and to new digital technologies.

nok heilmut

dubai emirates
dubai sports cit

sport and leisure

sport and leisure

Sports and leisure facilities are the most recent type of property development favored by the wealthy UAE. This is the new frontier of investment, which is currently being expanded in many areas of the country, absorbing a large part of its huge income from oil sales. Scrupulous care and attention is being dedicated to this, just as was the case with the development of the residential complexes, hotels, and infrastructure.

The great American and European firms specializing in this sector have been enlisted to design the new facilities, for which accreditation from the various international sports organizations is actively sought, with the aim of making them venues for the world's greatest sporting events and competitions (the country is preparing to bid for the Olympic Games).

Dubai, for example, already hosts the Dubai World Cup, one of the horse races with the richest purses in the world, as well as the soccer championship of the UAE's Etisalat National League. Abu Dhabi is home to a street circuit that has already hosted the first Formula One Festival, with cars driven by various racing stars, while the Abu Dhabi Grand Prix will be held from 2009 to 2016 on a 3.5-mile (5.5-km) state-of-the-art track on Yas Island, featuring permanent and non-permanent sections. The country's sports facilities and venues are among the most innovative and modern in the world, allowing the pursuit of all disciplines, including summer and winter sports, indoor and outdoor pursuits and water sports, with camel-racing tracks, indoor ski slopes, high-tech motor-racing tracks, elegant golf courses, luxurious indoor cricket pitches, and huge soccer stadiums.

The scale of the projects is always grandiose, nothing is left to chance and every structure is designed to draw astonished admiration before the first stone is even laid, attracting media attention from the international press. The developments are characterized by a two-fold philosophy, which is intended to equip the country with all the necessary facilities to improve the quality of life and leisure activities of the local population, while boosting international tourism by maximizing the level of hotel accommodation and tourist attractions. Thus venues designed to host international events will be flanked by sports academies destined to coach local youngsters and future champions (for example, the Manchester United Soccer

Schools, the Butch Harmon School of Golf, the David Lloyd Academy for tennis, and the International Global Cricket Academy in Dubai). The objective is pursued whatever the cost, altering the natural environment to the extent of using desalinated water (perhaps even more valuable than oil in this part of the world) to grass golf courses and employing vast amounts of energy to create artificial snow, all in an attempt to subjugate the fierce climate. Modern technologies are exploited to the full, with state-of-the-art materials, structures, and systems.

Water sports are widely practiced along the coast. Most of the facilities, such as diving centers or schools offering the necessary equipment for water skiing, sailing, and windsurfing, are part of the holiday packages offered by the luxury hotels and are not usually accessible to independent travelers. However, other activities are also available, such as camel treks in Al Ain, or jeep safaris in the desert (known as "wadi bashing") offered in Dubai and Sharjah.

Dubai is undoubtedly the leading emirate in the equally profitable sector of leisure and entertainment. Dubailand, covering an area of 107 sq miles (277 sq km), is destined to become the world's largest entertainment complex, offering an array of theme parks (water, educational, and wildlife) and sports areas, as well as a Formula One racetrack and numerous hotels and shopping malls.

Abu Dhabi will be the home of Acropolis Universe Resort designed by Behnisch Architekten, which will be an enormous leisure complex set in an artificial landscape characterized by a large purpose-built lake surrounded by lush vegetation. It will feature games areas, restaurants, movie theaters, auditoriums, parks and golf courses, dotted with enormous umbrella-like structures that modify the microclimate below, mitigating the high temperatures of the region. However, the greatest emphasis currently seems to be on the world of motoring. One of the star attractions of Dubai Sports City, currently under construction, will be Ferrari World, while in Abu Dhabi, the Dutch firm ONL is designing the huge Automotive Complex. In addition to a car museum, the complex will have restaurants, hotels, a design academy, conference center, showrooms exhibiting epoch-making marques, including Ferrari, Jaguar, BMW and Chrysler, and a series of test tracks for fast cars and SUVs. O.E.B.

Autodrome

DUBAI

Situated on a headland a 25-minute drive from the city center, the Dubai Autodrome is destined to become one of the world's great motor-sports and leisure attractions. Indeed, the new racing circuit for cars and motorbikes is part of a colossal urban development, which will also house new entertainment, sports, cultural, retail and leisure facilities, and residential units. The development is known as Dubailand and aims to become the world's leading entertainment complex, capable of competing with Walt Disney World Resort, which is currently the world's most famous and popular amusement park. Dubailand will feature multipurpose stadiums for all the most important sports, lush green golf courses, a snow-dome for skiers, a permanent exhibition of the art and culture of all

the countries in the world, an area dedicated to Arabian history and traditions, the Dubai Universal Studios, a space museum, a huge outlet mall, a water park, and much more besides. The complex will occupy an area of 107 sq miles (277 sq km), comprising 45 mega-projects and 200 sub-projects. It is the first time that such an unusual mixture of culture and entertainment will be located in the same place. Work commenced a couple of years ago and is expected to be completed between 2015 and 2018.

The Autodrome was designed by the American sports architecture firm of HOK Sport. It boasts a 3.35-mile (5.4-km) circuit with several possible configurations and a Business Park, which will be an executive center consisting of hotels and conference rooms.

236 top For this design, the HOK Sport architecture firm was inspired by the world of racing and engines. In their shape and materials used, each wing has been inspired by a race car's engine parts.

236 bottom Inclined spaces, protruding structural bodies, striking finishes, and metallic colors are employed to emphasize the automobile context of the racetrack. Speed, movement, and acceleration characterize the design of the entire structure.

237 The grandstand is the largest structure in the complex. It has an initial capacity of 7,000 seats, which can be enlarged up to 15,000. Defined by projecting bleachers, the incredible cantilevered roof also shelters spectators from the sun.

238-239 These luminous interiors were primarily finished with light-colored flooring, surfaces, and furnishings. Of paramount importance to the design were the views of the racetrack.

239 top The inclination given to volumes was studied to suggest the dynamic sense of speed, acceleration, and movement.

239 bottom Spatial orientation, aluminum fixtures, shades, and protective awnings all serve to guarantee shelter from the sun.

240-241 The Dubai Autodrome is equipped with all of the necessary facilities for a racetrack that aspires to become one of the great venues in the motor-sport world. It intends to accommodate every type of racing event in order to satisfy the Gulf states' citizens ever-increasing passion for speed and racing.

Autodrome

The circuit is already in use and is characterized by a combination of high-speed straights and technical bends, which make it spectacular and entertaining. In 2007, work commenced on the construction of the first Ferrari World, a theme park entirely dedicated to the Maranello-based car manufacturer. Highlights will include racing simulators, an interactive museum, and outlets selling the Italian company's merchandising line.

A full range of facilities has been built to complete the circuit: a commercial and administrative building, a pit complex, grandstands, a racing school, and a karting track. The architecture of the Autodrome is modern and original, with a design inspired by the world of motoring and racing. Metal surfaces, curved glass, overhanging parts, and sloping sections evoke the mechanical components or engine parts of a racing car. The result is extremely fluid and aerodynamic architecture based on the principle of dynamic equilibrium and achieved by an elegant formal solution that assiduously balances speed and traction, movement and control. The Autodrome's largest and most original structure is the grandstand, designed during the first stage of the project, with a capacity of 7,000 seats that can be increased to 15,000. This versatility also allows it to host concerts and other large public events.   O.E.B.

240 bottom and 241 bottom
The large windows facing onto the racetrack were manufactured with special double-paned, UV-protected glass, guaranteeing a good view and stopping the interiors from overheating. At night, the building is illuminated behind large windows that make this structure a beacon in the desert.

242 top and 242-243 This "ski resort" was created on the roof of the Emirates Mall, one of the largest in the world. From the outside, it appears to be a large steel tube without any exterior openings. Its form defines the width and creates the uneven levels of the ski runs.

Ski Dubai Emirates Mall

DUBAI

The new Dubai, expanding at a dizzy rate on the edge of the desert with its ceaseless creation of increasingly ambitious and innovative projects, also has room for a few oddities. In a place where bulldozers and ships can be seen continuously shifting sand for the construction of artificial islands with unusual shapes, and where the construction of the world's tallest skyscraper is currently underway, an indoor ski resort has been built. Defying all climatic and environmental logic, a huge metal construction has been erected to house a painstakingly re-created mountain slope, kept permanently snow-covered all year round. Ski Dubai, with over 240,000 sq ft (22,300 sq m) of snowy ski slopes, is one of the most peculiar and unique facilities in Dubai. The resort is part of the Emirates Mall, one of the largest shopping malls in the world, covering a total area of 2.4 million sq ft (223,000 sq m) and housing 450 stores, a 14-cinema complex, and 70 restaurants.

Inaugurated in November 2005, Ski Dubai is the Middle East's first indoor ski resort. It is situated just a short taxi ride from the beach and the celebrated seven-star Burj Al Arab hotel. This masterpiece of engineering boasts five ski runs of varying difficulty and length. The longest is more than 1,300 ft (400 m) with a fall of over 200 ft (60 m). Its facilities include a quad chairlift that carries skiers to the top of the main run, a ski carpet that serves the nursery slope, and a tow lift. The setting and atmosphere are made even more realistic by a mid-station, a fully equipped chalet for relaxing breaks, a ski school that organizes individual and group courses for children and adults, as well as mounds, moguls and troughs, with strategically placed pine trees. In short, everything that you could possibly wish for to ski like a professional in the desert. The facilities are completed by a 295-ft (90-m) quarter pipe and a Freestyle Zone, as well as an adjoining 3,200-sq-ft (300-sq-m) Snow Park with a

snowball-throwing gallery, toboggan runs, a snow cavern, and a play area where children can have fun and climb the observation tower at the bottom of the main slope.

The indoor ski resort has a maximum capacity of 1,500 people and the entrance ticket includes rental of all the necessary equipment and clothing for all types of winter sports. Fully equipped changing rooms allow visitors to swap their summer clothing for warm skiwear. Any missing gear can be conveniently purchased from the well-stocked store inside the complex. Several themed restaurants are situated on the ski runs, whose colored lights and plastic-looking pine trees give them a vaguely Christmassy atmosphere. The mid-station of the chair lift is home to the Avalanche Café, while the curved run boasts the St. Moritz Café.

In order to ensure at least 20 inches (50 cm) of compact snow and the appropriate atmosphere of a winter mountainside, each day over 6,500 tons (5,900 tonnes) of snow at a constant temperature of 28°F (-2°C) are blasted from the snow cannons suspended from the roof. The unique effect can be observed through a huge window separating the entrance of the Mall of the Emirates from the indoor ski resort.

243 Ski Dubai is an incredible artificial re-creation of a "winter" resort. The complex covers an area almost the size of three soccer fields, terraced in such a way as to stabilize the "snow" cover. A day on the snow is made all the better by enjoyable breaks in the restaurants and shops. Ski equipment may be rented easily, while balconies and large windows allow spectators to follow the exploits of the skiers and snowboarders enjoying their exhilarating day's sport on the desert's "snow." The ski runs are also equipped with "mid-mountain refuges" that allow tourists to take a break and grab some refreshments.

244-245 and 244 bottom
The environment that has been created is a microcosm of an alpine scene with fog, fresh snow, wooden huts, and snowcapped fir trees. This re-creation has been superbly achieved.

From the outside Ski Dubai resembles a huge metal tube supported by a framework of steel beams, which gleams in the blazing desert sun without revealing its peculiar function. The success of indoor skiing in the Emirates has been so great that plans are already underway for the opening of the Dubai Sunny Mountain Ski Dome, which will even feature a revolving ski slope. It will be situated in the colossal Dubailand leisure complex currently being built just outside the city. O.E.B.

245 top For those who do not like to ski, other activities such as tobogganing and snowboarding are available. Visitors may rent all the necessary equipment to spend a day enjoying winter sports.

245 bottom An efficient three-seat chairlift runs over cabling supports anchored to the roof and ensures a quick trip to the top of the ski runs, which vary in length and level of difficulty.

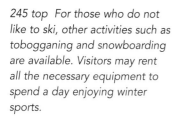

Dubai Sports City

DUBAI

GMP ARCHITEKTEN VON GERKAN
MARG UND PARTNER

In the Emirates the desire to build the biggest and most amazing structures is not restricted to residential developments, but also involves the world of sport, as exemplified by Dubai Sports City. This proposed huge urban complex will cover an area of over 50 million sq ft (4,650,00 sq m) and will almost entirely be dedicated to sport and will be an integral part of the larger and even more ambitious urban project of Dubailand, which will be the world's largest leisure and entertainment park.

Dubai Sports City will be the first purpose-built sports city, which will not only feature facilities for all sports, at both amateur and professional levels, but also residential and commercial developments, schools, places of worship, private clinics, community facilities and green areas. It will thus offer an efficient and specialized base for sporting associations and an ideal venue for international sports events. The design of the complex was inspired by the most advanced modern metropolises, where sport becomes a lifestyle, merging with the urban layout of a traditional city. It will offer comfortable living and will be ideal for the training of the athletes of the future, destined to become the legends of a modern society.

The site of the complex is almost square and is bounded by highways, including Al Khail Road and Emirates Road, which run towards the coast and the famous Jumeirah Beach resort. The western side of the plot houses areas mainly destined for commercial and residential use. There are two main types of residential developments: a large sector with extensive green areas and golf courses, featuring detached and semidetached villas (Gallery Villas) in a sort of garden city; and five multistory buildings housing apartments (Canal Residence).

However, the throbbing heart of Dubai Sports City will be the area housing the sports facilities, arranged around a large lake. All the venues have been designed to the specifications of the international governing bodies for the relevant sports. The facilities, distinguished by their original structural design and unusual forms, will host major international events in soccer, cricket, rugby, golf, hockey, tennis, and many other sports. Dubai Sports City will also be home to top-level sports academies and schools.

The cricket stadium will have the capacity for 25,000 spectators, which can be expanded to 30,000, and state-of-the-art facilities for players, match officials, and the media. It will be one of the most advanced grounds in the world, thanks to the involvement of the International Cricket Council

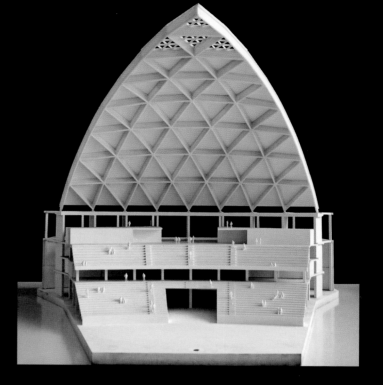

246-247 This large soccer stadium is characterized by a triangular lightweight roof that shades the public space and the maintenance and service machinery and other facilities installed beneath the stands.

247 top left The main sports complex forms an arch around an artificial lake, creating a cluster consisting of four facilities equipped and ready to host events of any of the major sports.

247 top right This section of the small-scale model houses a covered sports facility. The equilateral triangle motif is important to Arabic cultural tradition and it recurs over the louvered waffle slab roof of the grandstand structure.

GMP ARCHITEKTEN VON GERKAN
MARG UND PARTNER

248 The soccer stadium's design may be interpreted as the sum of a series of distinct parts: the playing field, the grandstand accommodating spectators, the spaces for facilities carved out beneath the grandstand, the perimeter foundational ring, the roofing support system, and the roof's surface finish.

249 top This is a photorealistic rendering of the stadium's interior from where you can see the grandstand, the playing field, and the eight-lane track for international track and field competitions.

249 bottom These long profiles and cross sections demonstrate the primary features of this installation conceived in a large, partly subterranean basin. The stadium has a regulation size grass playing field for high level competitions, three grandstands of equal size to accommodate thousands of fans, a large roof with a sawtooth profile made from special fabrics to protect spectators from the sun, parking areas, locker rooms, workout areas, and shops beneath the grandstands.

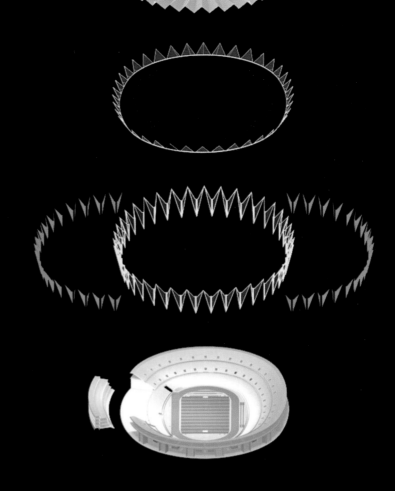

at every stage of the design process. An indoor arena with a capacity of 10,000 will be dedicated to sports such as basketball, volleyball, ice hockey, and handball, but it can also host cultural events, exhibitions, and concerts, while an outdoor stadium with a capacity of 60,000 will offer a venue for soccer and rugby games, athletic competitions, and outdoor shows and concerts. There will also be an outdoor hockey field with seating for 5,000 spectators, and The Dunes, an 18-hole golf course, designed by international golf star Ernie Els, which is set to become one of the finest courses in the Middle East.

The form of the structures in this complex, designed by the German architecture firm of Gerkan, Marg und Partner, is derived from the combination of traditional Arabian architecture, closely linked to the climate and the local culture, with modern membrane roof systems, which make the purpose of the buildings absolutely explicit. Geometric forms – principally triangles – are used to build the frameworks but also as the figurative motifs that characterize the structures.   O.E.B.

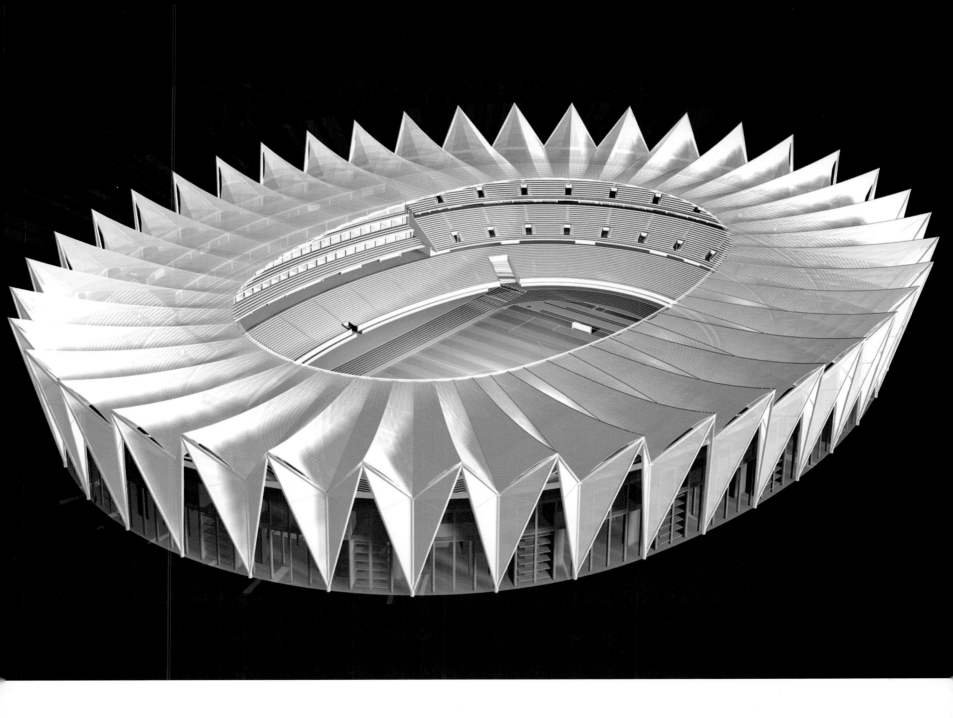

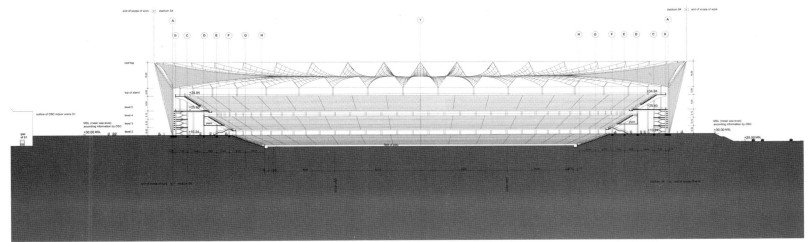

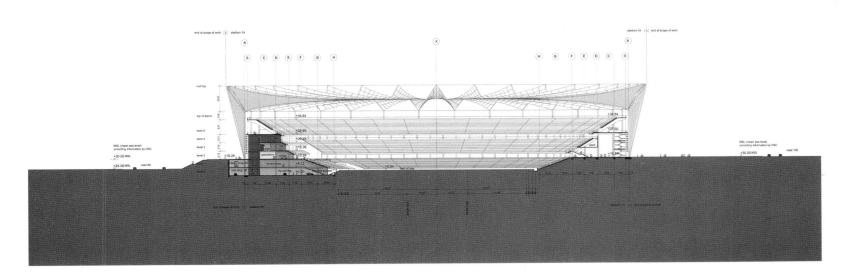

mjm (international convention centre) - za

bridge) - ws atkins & partners (metr

public buildings
and infrastructure

ha hadid & associates *(sheikh*

public buildings and infrastructure

The urban expansion of an area is closely related to the development of its infrastructure. Sheikh Zayed Road illustrates this point well, because in a short space of time it has gone from a simple desert track to the main highway connecting the UAE to the other countries of the Arabian Peninsula. The urban stretch of the road is now lined by the bristling forest of skyscrapers that are part of the rapidly expanding metropolitan area of Dubai, resembling a new Manhattan. This district has made the city world famous and is home to its most prestigious commercial developments, such as the Dubai International Finance Centre. The very layout and urban identity of the city is based on the main junctions of Sheikh Zayed Road.

Sheikh Zayed Bridge is the third bridge to connect the island of Abu Dhabi to the mainland and is part of an infrastructure network designed to expand and improve communications with the other emirates. Although the geography of this stretch of coast, characterized by a string of closely spaced islands rising from a lagoon, represents an important resource for tourism due to the availability of waterfront sites, it also poses several problems in terms of connecting the new urban developments. At least ten bridges are planned to ensure access to the new areas, including those focusing on Al Reem Island and Saadiyat Island.

The development of the entire coast, which increasingly resembles a huge linear city, is proceeding at a dizzying rate and requires large-scale replanning of the area's infrastructure. Despite the availability of space and wide highways, traffic has started to become a problem as a result of a population boom with one of the highest growth rates in the world, well over 5 per cent. This is compounded by the many visitors who enter the country, both for tourism and for business. Indeed, the Dubai Development and Investment Authority (DDIA) aims to attract 15 million tourists in 2010, almost three times the 2003 figure. Consequently, the public transport network (currently offering road services only) must be planned and expanded. The number of buses and both urban and inter-urban routes increases each year. Dubai's new elevated light railway network, commenced in the late 1990s, also aims to tackle the problem, taking into consideration estimated future traffic volumes. The imminent inauguration of the two lines currently under construction will mark another world record, namely that of the longest completely automated network. In 2007 the Road and Transport Authority announced the commencement of work on the third of the four lines planned.

Abu Dhabi, the country's capital, is also planning a rail network, which will feature both high-speed trains that will stop at several key stations in the city before continuing to Dubai, and interconnecting freight lines. The network has been designed as an integrated transport system offering local services and also connecting the seven emirates and extending beyond the country's borders. The port system and merchant shipping, which have long been two of the country's most developed resources, are continuously being expanded and modernized. The airport network in particular is being upgraded to strengthen the UAE's geographic status as a hub between East and West, and its role as both an economic gateway to the new Asian financial markets and as a cultural melting pot. The announcement of the possible location of a new spaceport for suborbital tourist flights in the emirate of Ras Al Khaimah will extend the reach of the country's transport infrastructure into space.

In terms of design, it is vital that the public transport system, trains, and stations take account of the country's particular climate, because the average temperature reaches 113 °F (45 °C) in summer, making outdoor activities practically impossible. All public functions are performed in air-conditioned indoor areas, greatly influencing urban design and generating high energy costs. The strategic planning of the UAE is aimed at dealing with urban and demographic growth and at the expansion of the primary urbanization networks, identifying objectives for sustainable development and protecting the local environment and ecosystems. Government policy is not only engaged in establishing limits for energy consumption and resources for buildings, but also intends to lay the bases for concrete economic and commercial development and for research in these areas. Although this awareness is a very recent development – the Masdar Initiative is a pilot project in this respect – several experimental projects have already been implemented in the field of alternative energy, focusing chiefly on wind and solar power. Solar energy in particular has been considered for use in the desalination plants to treat seawater, which constitutes the country's main water source. L.D.

International Convention Centre

DUBAI

The location of the Dubai International Convention and Exhibition Centre (DICEC) allows visitors to admire two contrasting images of the city, because it is strategically located between the glittering skyscrapers, built thanks to the emirate's recent international economic and financial success, and the souks, old buildings, and bustle of the city's historic district. It is part of a complex that also features residential buildings, two hotels, several parking lots (including one multistory one) and the Dubai World Trade Centre, a 39-story office tower built in 1979, which has become one of Dubai's most prominent landmarks. The Dubai International Convention and Exhibition Centre offers a huge area of flexible, multipurpose spaces suitable for hosting the a diverse range of cultural events, meetings, and exhibitions.

The center has an irregular L-shaped plan, along which the various exhibition spaces are arranged. These are accessible from a path that connects the two ends of the complex and is known by different names. Thus the Za'abeel Concourse leads to the Za'abeel conference hall, before becoming Concourse 1 and connecting four other halls arranged along a single side. The junction between Concourse 1 and Concourse 2 coincides with the Exhibition Gate, which is the entrance to the Exhibition Centre on Sheikh Zayed Road. A rounded recess in the long glass façade marks this entrance. A further six multipurpose halls line Concourse 2, while the center's second entrance is the Convention Gate, facing the opposite direction to the Exhibition Gate and characterized by ornamental panels with arabesque motifs.

254 left The Dubai International Convention and Exhibition Centre is located just a short distance from the World Trade Centre, an iconic building that exemplifies the landscape of the city, and also the first skyscraper built in this commercial district of Dubai.

254 right Convention Tower rises up alongside Convention Gate. Its square design is 15 stories high, accommodating spaces intended for international conventions and meeting rooms for high-level businesspeople.

255 This façade is made up of a combination of materials: large windows provide light to shared hallways, modular patterned panels comprise the opaque enclosure, and metallic shading elements regulate incoming sunlight.

International
Convention
Centre

The Convention Tower and the Novotel stand either side of this gateway.

Long indoor corridors lined with stores, banks, post offices, real-estate brokers, restaurants, and cafés connect the various halls. They also lead to the entrances of the complex's two hotels. All the areas can be easily reached and have been designed to eliminate architectural barriers, making them accessible to all categories of users.

All the halls along Concourse 1 and Concourse 2 can be divided using soundproof partitions if required. This enables the creation of up to 18 meeting rooms, each seating from 50 to 220 people. The 82,914-sq-ft (7,700-sq-m) Sheikh Rashid Hall and the 41,280-sq-ft (3,835-sq-m) Sheikh Maktoum Hall can be joined to form a huge conference hall able to seat 12,000 people. The nine interconnecting exhibition halls are located on the ground floor. They have free floor plans, unobstructed by columns, and cover a total area of 646,000 sq ft (60,000 sq m).

The elegant Al Multaqua Ballroom can accommodate up to 600 people for exclusive events. Its neo-Arabian style makes it the ideal setting for wedding banquets, cocktail parties, exhibitions, and receptions, but it can also be transformed into a conference hall able to seat 1,000 people. O.E.B.

256 The Dubai International Convention and Exhibition Centre rises up within an urban landscape that contains other important commercial buildings, notably the landmark World Trade Centre, the Novotel, and the Ibis Hotel, as well as various residential developments.

257 The entrance corridor to Concourse 2 stands at double height and is illuminated with zenithal light through a large skylight installed in the roof. The convention rooms open onto the sides while the Convention Gate and Exhibition Gate are situated at the end.

Sheikh Zayed Bridge

ABU DHABI

Abu Dhabi's great urban expansion necessitates the upgrading of the infrastructure connecting it to the other emirates and the countries of the southern coast of the Persian Gulf along the Sheikh Zayed Road. The Sheikh Zayed Bridge will be the third bridge to span the narrow strait between the island on which the capital stands and the mainland. The first bridge was made of steel and was built in 1967. It was followed in the 1970s by a second bridge, located further south.

This third bridge, designed by Zaha Hadid, will allow access to the city and will play a key role in the development and completion of the highway system and so has been dubbed the Gateway Crossing. It will be positioned in an open setting at the northern end of the strait, and its iconic form will be an attraction in itself and also a catalyst for further development. The bridge's design is based on the fluid dynamic lines that are the British-Iraqi architect's hallmark, and on her personal interpretation of the complex relations and functions of the contemporary world. A collection of structures, forming the spine of the bridge, rises from the mainland shore before plunging towards the water and re-emerging to a height of almost 200 ft (60 m) and proceeding towards the city with a sinusoidal waveform.

The three arches, the largest of which has a span of 768 ft (234 m), are continued in the curved support structures. They form undulating lines that intersect and split, diverging under the road decks to the outside of the roadways, each of which will carry five lanes, plus an emergency one and a pedestrian path. The overall effect of the steel and reinforced concrete bridge (2,762 ft/842 m long and 223 ft/68 m wide) is of an imposing yet elegant sculptural work thanks to the sense of movement inherent in the design. The two road decks are made from reinforced concrete sections, each 79 ft (24 m) wide and 18 ft (5.5 m) thick. The road runs 66 ft (20 m) above sea level, supported by mass concrete piers and suspended by cables from the steel

arches. These arches are made from hollow sections measuring up to 26 by 20 ft (8 by 6 m) and up to 3.5 inches (9 cm) thick.

The bridge rests on four foundations in the water, two piers on land, and with two heads at either end. The unique design – symmetrical in width but not in length – required precise three-dimensional modeling and simulation to test its structural integrity not only during normal use, but also in the event of natural hazards, such as earthquakes, or if it was struck by a ship. L.D.

258-259 Seen here from the land side, the bridge is built with two structures over which the divided highway runs, providing a quick link to and from the island of Abu Dhabi.

259 bottom This view from the island side shows clearly the wave-like lines of the bridge's support system, which first run to the inside then to the outside of the divided highway.

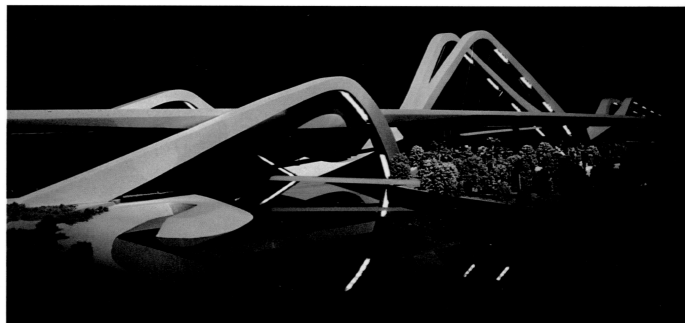

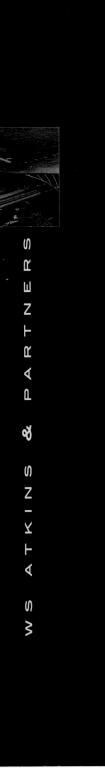

Metro

DUBAI

Currently experiencing rampant economic and urban expansion and rapidly becoming a tourist mecca, Dubai's population is expected to reach 3 million by 2017, with tourist numbers projected to hit 15 million by 2010. Consequently, the emirate has had to take action aimed at solving the expected traffic congestion problems.

As early as 1997, studies carried out by Dubai Municipality recommended the creation of a metropolitan public transport network as a possible solution to the city's spasmodic development.

International engineering firm WS Atkins & Partners was commissioned to coordinate and oversee the civil engineering works required to construct the first two lines (the Red Line and the Green Line), including tunnels, viaducts, stations, depots, the actual railways, and all the related services. The coordination of the work also involves other aspects, including the reduction of the project's environmental impact, fire safety, signaling, and similar technical considerations. As the Dubai Metro is one of the largest infrastructure projects under construction in the world, this is an extremely complicated task.

The first two lines will have a total length of 46.5 miles (75 km), with several underground stretches and the rest on elevated viaducts carefully designed to integrate with the urban fabric. The lines will not cross any of the existing highways. The three depots and 44 stations (including ten underground ones) boast an

260-261 Dubai's elevated train stations are enclosed and air-conditioned to guard against excessive overheating. A dynamically accentuated curvilinear surface makes up the enclosure of this station.

261 The metropolitan train network is elevated on a viaduct with the exception of the tunnel that passes below Dubai Creek. To minimize the detrimental impact on the surrounding area, environmental measures were included in the urban planning stages.

WS ATKINS & PARTNERS

elegant rational design characterized by a curved roof that follows the rails, emphasizing their direction. Stations at the junctions of the two lines will have taxi ranks and car parks.

The longest line is the Red Line, scheduled to open in 2009. It commences at Jebel Ali Port and passes under the Creek to reach Dubai International Airport and beyond, following a course parallel to the coast.

The Green Line has an almost circular form and links the two strategic locations of Healthcare City and the Airport Free Zone, intersecting the Red Line at two points. All the stations are indoors, allowing them to be air-conditioned and offer high security.

The driverless, fully automated trains will also be air-conditioned and comprise five cars seating 400 passengers, including separate sections for women and children and a first-class section for VIPs. One of the key objectives of the construction phase, commenced in 2006, is to minimize the impact on traffic and city life, particularly during excavation.

Two further lines, the Blue Line and the Purple Line, are planned for the future. They will connect the existing Dubai International Airport with the new Dubai World Central International Airport, which is part of an enormous terminal under construction near Jebel Ali.

By 2020, it is estimated that the entire network will extend for 197.5 miles (318 km) and have an average capacity of 1.2 million passengers per day, which could be further increased by a supplementary light railway system.   L.D.

planning

planning

The urban expansion of the UAE is driven by the initiatives of leading international property developers, both private and state-owned, which act on a global scale and principally in the Middle East. The great new urbanization projects are astounding in terms of scale and the rapidity with which they are devouring the desert. They concentrate on two strictly related investment targets, namely the creation of new tourist resorts and the planning and building of new infrastructure and facilities aimed at boosting both tourism and business. In the first case, the key factor is location, which contributes to increasing property values. The most sought-after sites are undoubtedly waterfront plots, which not only ensure exclusive views, but also allow potential access directly from the sea, as well as the possibility of equipping the shore with luxurious private beaches and marinas. The same overriding theme has inspired imposing works of marine engineering in Dubai, such as the three artificial Palm Islands and the new archipelago known as The World, along with other projects such as Dubai Marina and Business Bay, which extends the Creek.

Two opposite approaches have been adopted for the problem of building new residential and tourist developments on the waterfront. The first of these is the artificial extension of the coastline by hundreds of miles using rock and sand dredged from the seafloor. The second is the excavation of artificial basins and channels in the desert. Abu Dhabi is situated on a group of islands a few hundred yards off the mainland and so has a clear advantage in this respect. The city, whose expansion was initially directed towards the mainland, is now planning the urban development of the nearby islands, which are currently almost deserted, with projects such as those for Al Reem Island and Saadiyat Island. The latter development, involving some of the most illustrious names in contemporary architecture, features cultural venues designed by the world's foremost architects that are destined to become not only a source of national pride and prestige, but also international attractions, on the model of Bilbao.

The emirate of Ras Al Khaimah boasts the country's most breathtakingly beautiful natural scenery and has pinpointed the striking mountain range that occupies part of its territory as a potential tourist destination offering a valid alternative to coastal sites. The other aspect of urban planning, which is not concentrated exclusively on residential and hotel facilities, is constituted principally by new service areas, such as Dubai Media City, where the creation of a communications, information, and television entertainment district has been promoted by offering fiscal benefits and fiber-optic cabling, or the prestigious Dubai International Finance Centre, which houses all the functions and activities of the country's burgeoning financial economy. These developments are flanked by new ones, which combine tourist attractions with residential and hotel areas. An emblematic example is Dubailand, the world's largest amusement complex, packed with attractions. The huge urban project, covering an area of around 70,000 acres (28,000 hectares), is divided into seven theme parks, comprising innovative entertainment venues and attractions of all kinds on a spectacular scale. They include a fun fair and an educational nature reserve, along with sports venues of all kinds, and what is billed as the world's largest shopping mall.

Almost all of these projects are completely new to the region, because the area was characterized by only small desert settlements until the end of the 1970s and also due to the nomadic culture of the country, which has no established urban traditions. One of the few exceptions is Abu Dhabi's Aldar Central Market, which nonetheless requires the demolition and reconstruction of an area formerly occupied by the traditional souk. In the absence of an existing urban fabric and a larger city planning scheme, the new settlements tend to grow up independently as isolated clusters and enclaves, following the waterfront or a landscaping approach, without any real urban plan. The elegant Dubai International Finance Centre constitutes a unique exception, for it is arranged along a main axis marked by a monumental entrance portal known as The Gate, designed by Gensler in an explicit tribute to Paris' Arc de Triomphe.

Foster + Partners' recent projects inspired by the close-knit fabric of the Islamic city are not so much a celebration of the cultural region to which the country belongs as a recognition of an urban solution perfected over the centuries to adapt to the climate of its surroundings. Indeed, the great new theme of urban expansion in the emirates – among the world's leading producers of hydrocarbons – is environmental sustainability.

As the projects involve the creation of entire city districts, it is possible to introduce the theme in every aspect of their construction and management, while simultaneously implementing economic policy as in the case of the Masdar Initiative. Here, too, Abu Dhabi appears to be drawing on the more advanced experiences of Dubai.   L.D.

THE PALM TRILOGY AND THE WORLD

VARIOUS AUTHORS

AS THE COUNTRY'S MOST LUCRATIVE AND SOUGHT-AFTER AREAS FOR TOURISM DEVELOPMENT ARE LOCATED ON THE SEAFRONT, OR AT LEAST CLOSE TO THE WATER, THE GOVERNMENT-OWNED AL NAKHEEL PROPERTIES IS CREATING AN ARRAY OF ARTIFICIAL ISLANDS TO EXTEND DUBAI'S COASTLINE AND BOOST ITS REAL ESTATE MARKET.

The Palm Jumeirah, commenced in 2001, is the first of the three Palm Islands (the others are the Palm Jebel Ali and the Palm Deira). Situated just off the coast of Dubai, these will be the largest artificial islands in the world, built from sand dredged from the bottom of the Persian Gulf. Their particular shape not only maximizes beach area, but also gives them a specific identity. Indeed, the islands have the form of a stylized palm tree, with the trunk close to the mainland and the symmetrically arranged fronds reaching out into the Gulf. A circular breakwater has been built around each of the islands to protect them from the sea. Conceived as an international tourist attraction, they will be home to a mixture of low- and medium-density residential buildings, luxury hotels, and leisure and entertainment facilities. The areas on the nearby mainland, to which they are connected by bridges, are also being developed with prestigious buildings and complexes and they will become access portals to the islands.

The Palm Jumeirah has already been completed. It has 17 fronds and measures roughly 3 miles (5 km) across and 3 miles (5 km) in length, with a 48-mile (77-km) coastline. It is characterized by the two Logo

Islands in the shape of the development's symbol (a palm leaf) lying either side of its trunk. The Palm Jebel Ali also has 17 fronds, although it is approximately 50 percent larger than the Palm Jumeirah, with 62 miles (100 km) of coast. Villas raised on piles will be built inside the breakwater, along with a water theme park with boardwalks arranged to form a writing in Arabic. The Palm Deira, commenced in 2004, is the largest of the

three islands, with an overall area of 31 sq miles (80 sq km) and 140 miles (225 km) of beaches. The initial design, which featured 41 fronds, has been modified and scaled down following detailed technical studies.

The characteristic form of the Palm Islands advertises the development on a global scale. Indeed, the islands are visible from airplanes and satellites, whose images can be accessed by anyone through Google

266-267 This satellite image has been altered to show Dubai's coastline when all anticipated development has been completed. From right, Palm Deira, the World, Palm Jumeirah, and Palm Jebel Ali, around which is the arc of the Dubai Waterfront.

Earth. The same promotional idea informed the design and construction of The World, an archipelago of 300 artificial islands constructed in the shape of a world map surrounded by a breakwater and located 2.5 miles (4 km) off the coast of Dubai.

The iconic stature of the project, which has an area of 3.5 sq miles (9 sq km) and 114 miles (183 km) of shoreline, is boosted by the patriotic and symbolic values associated with the countries that the individual islands represent. Indeed, the media hype has targeted a multimillionaire clientele of companies, politicians, film stars, and sports celebrities to sell them islands with the names and relative geographical positions of the world's various nations. The areas and coasts of the islands can be customized and developed by their owners according to a master plan.

On the basis of the international success of these projects, Al Nakheel Properties has also presented the plans for Dubai Waterfront and, at the beginning of 2008, The Universe. Dubai Waterfront, currently under construction, is situated west of the Palm Jebel Ali, near the border with Abu Dhabi.

The development consists of artificial islands shaped in an arc, which will cover an area of over 150 sq miles (388 sq km) with a coastline of more than 40 miles (64 km). The project also includes a harbor and the Arabian Canal, which is approximately 45 miles (72 km) long and will run from the coast into the desert. There will be 250 multipurpose complexes designed according to the principles of sustainable development and able to house an estimated population of 1.5 million people. The Universe will be an archipelago of artificial islands and is still at the planning stage. It will represent a map of the solar system, to be built between the Palm Jumeirah and The World. L.D.

Palm Jebel Ali

DUBAI

268 top right Island development will incorporate both high-rise and low-rise construction, and three different types of single family villas (Signature Villas, Garden Homes, and Canal Cove Town Homes).

268 top left Palm Jebel Ali is still under construction. Currently being built is the crescent, a semi-circular band that will surround and protect the central part of the palm tree from the sea currents.

268 bottom left Where the symmetrical "palm frond" spaces open, Palm Jebel Ali's central "trunk" section is practically a promontory, connected to the mainland only by roadways. The semi-circular crescent itself is directly linked to the coastline at either end.

268-269 At Palm Jumeirah, the crescent form is interrupted frequently to allow the circulation of water, while two symmetrical private islands flanking the "trunk" form the Al Nakheel Properties logo.

Palm Jumeirah

DUBAI

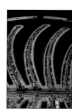

269 top Each of the 17 Palm Jumeirah "fronds" will house low-rise buildings that face directly onto the water, distributed off of a central road that branches off of the "palm tree's trunk."

270-271 At the north end of the "trunk," residential construction of the Marina Residences anticipates high-rise apartment buildings that will face directly onto the port of IGY Anchor Marina.

271 Managed by Island Global Yachting and accommodating more than 700 luxury yachts, the Anchor Marina offers exclusive services to pleasure craft owners, including restaurants, commercial spaces, and a clubhouse.

Palm Jumeirah

272 top The spectacular atrium of the Trump International Hotel & Tower represents the natural continuation of commercial and recreational structures along the Golden Mile, a street network that crosses through the long part of Palm Jumeirah's "trunk."

272 bottom Designed by the London-based multinational engineering and design consultancy, WS Atkins & Partners, the lower part of this building accommodates offices, residences, and a hotel, opening onto an entrance one floor above street level.

273 The rigid frame, portal-type skyscraper of the Trump International Hotel & Tower is 48 stories high and the monumental central element of Palm Jumeirah's "trunk." Two towers unite in the sky lobby where guests can enjoy impressive views of the island.

The World
DUBAI

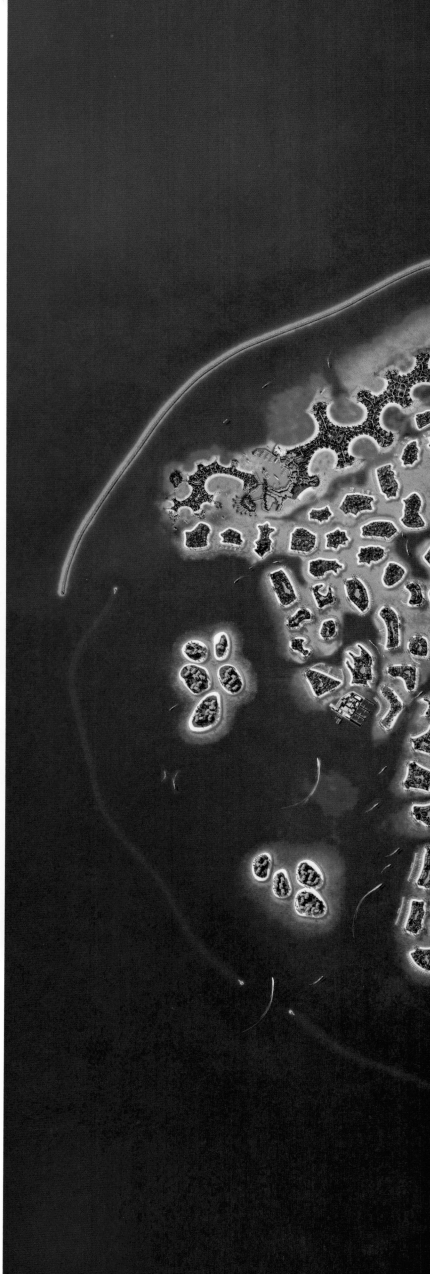

274 top The islands making up the World are sold along with a portion of the surrounding water. The buyer is free to model his or her own coastline within the framework of a predefined rule system, creating beaches, docks, and inlets.

274 bottom The archipelago is made up of not only private islands but also some that are public. The latter are centrally located with commercial buildings, transport facilities, and tourist resorts.

274-275 The cartographic representation of the earth at the World has been created by islands forming the outlines of the continents. This archipelago is surrounded by a circular barrier reef that protects it from sea currents.

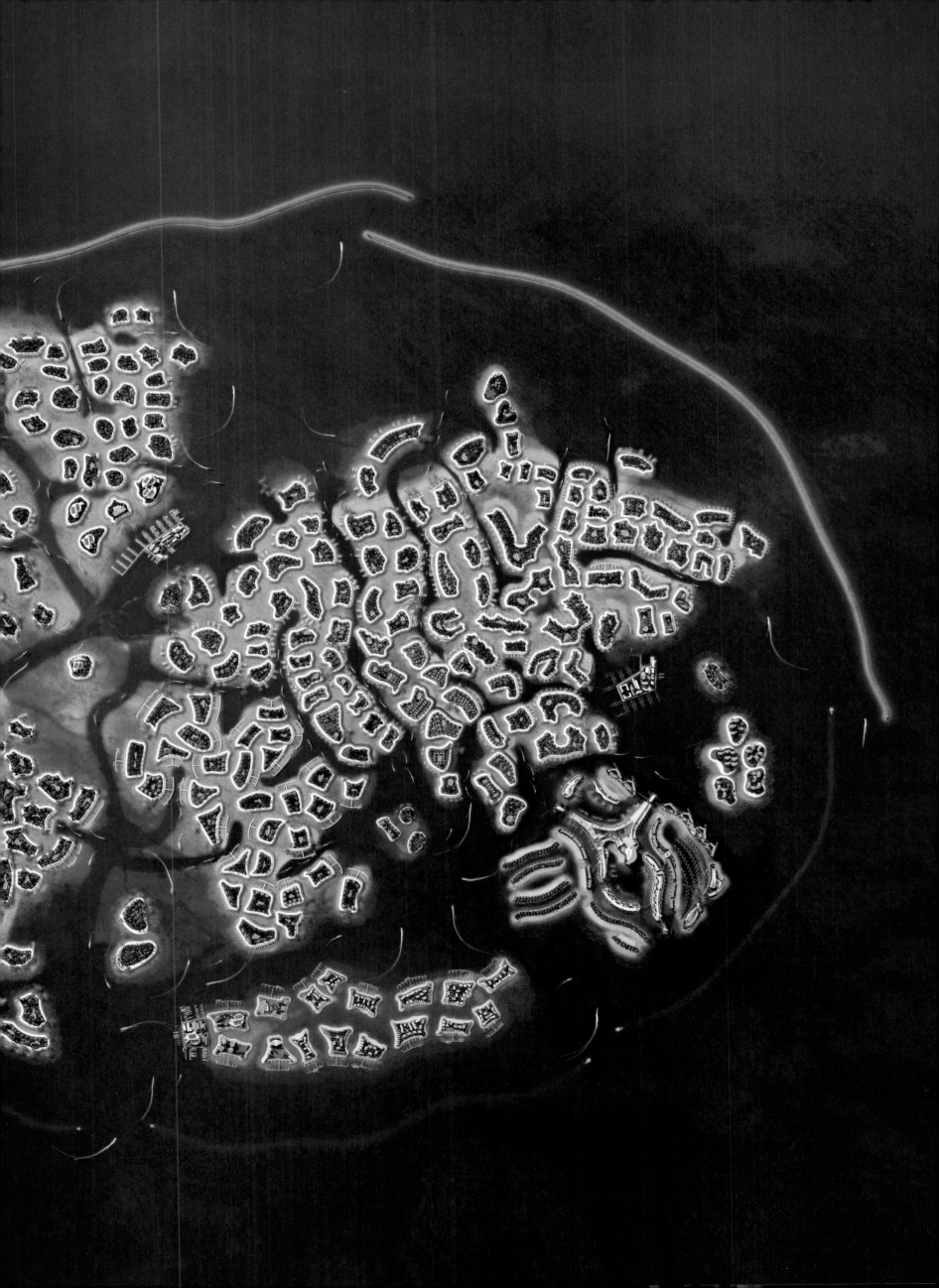

276-277 The Palm Deira development is more complex than the other Palm Islands. In addition to taking the form of a palm tree, it also includes other new coastal islands that embellish the functional plan of the project.

Palm Deira

DUBAI

277 top Representing the initial phase of the entire Palm Deira development, Deira Island facilities include a tourist port, Vibrant Marina, with amenities and services that will enhance the value of the residential complex overlooking it.

277 bottom In the middle of Deira Island, Cosmopolitan Boulevard is a pedestrian promenade with commercial units, restaurants, and cafés. The skyscraper anticipated for the base of the Palm Deira "trunk" will be the central icon of this area.

276 bottom In particular, Deira Island is the point of access to Palm Deira. A multifunction development is planned, organized around a wide pedestrian boulevard facing onto a promenade with recreational facilties.

Aldar Central Market

ABU DHABI

Central Market is an urban redevelopment project in central Abu Dhabi, covering an area of around 12 acres (5 hectares) between Khalifa Street, Airport Road, and Hamdan Street. The buildings currently under construction will replace the old Central Souk, which was demolished in 2005 and was the city's traditional market for over 40 years, particularly during the 1960s. The goal of the project, to be built by local developer Alder Properties PJSC, is to create a modern attraction that represents the pulsating heart of the metropolis, in terms of both its well-established financial activities and its burgeoning tourism industry, which is also capable of redeveloping the entire surrounding area. More generally, it aims to satisfy the needs of a city undergoing rapid economic development that attracts a constantly increasing number of tourists as it prepares to follow the more advanced expansion of nearby Dubai.

The project was awarded to the British architecture practice of Foster + Partners, who proposed a complex with close-knit, low-rise buildings designed for pedestrian access, with streets, lanes, squares and open spaces, and three tall towers to express its central role in the wider cityscape and on the city's skyline. The towers will contain of a 52-story, luxury five-star hotel with 250 rooms and 200 serviced apartments, a 58-story office building called WorkCentral, and the 88-story LiveCentral building housing 525 luxury residential units with one to four bedrooms, including duplexes, triplexes, and penthouses.

The public facilities in the low-rise structures of the complex (ShopCentral) will be split into two main areas. The first of these will consist of a shopping mall with department stores and prestigious boutiques, while the second will

278-279 Demolished to accommodate new construction, the design of the old, traditional souq is reintroduced in this new complex selling the same typical local merchandise, from food products to hand-crafted artisan items.

279 top Offices of international companies are housed in the structure's commercial zones. This project involves a modern interpretation of the latticework typical of Islamic architecture.

279 bottom Within the complex, screened open and closed spaces alternate horizontally and vertically, with wooden latticework that reintroduces the shielding technique of traditional mashrabiya (projecting oriel windows).

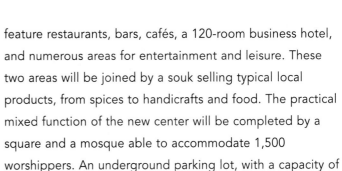

280-281 Three towers assume a distinctive and iconic role within this urban context, silhouetted against the Abu Dhabi skyline, and are the site for a hotel, offices, and luxury apartments.

feature restaurants, bars, cafés, a 120-room business hotel, and numerous areas for entertainment and leisure. These two areas will be joined by a souk selling typical local products, from spices to handicrafts and food. The practical mixed function of the new center will be completed by a square and a mosque able to accommodate 1,500 worshippers. An underground parking lot, with a capacity of 5,250 vehicles, will serve the entire complex.

Foster's formal language emphasizes the contrast between the modernity of the towers and the reworking of traditional forms in the low-rise buildings. The former, distinguished by their height and position, have an irregular elongated plan. Each of the towers is wrapped in an undulating skin resembling a softly draped fabric, which is suspended above street level and ends in a sloping roof.

The entire area around the towers will be occupied by juxtaposed parallelepipeds of different heights, ranging from two to five or six floors, some of which will be raised on *pilotis* above a four-sided base grid. Their exterior will be clad with wooden shutters, whose geometric arrangement of horizontal and vertical slats offers a modern interpretation of the traditional *mashrabiyas* that often characterize the windows of Islamic architecture. However, the purpose of these elements is not simply decorative or evocative, for they have preserved the original function of shading the building from the sun. This design solution has been employed horizontally as well as vertically, with sliding screens that allow the natural ventilation of the interiors. Once again, Norman Foster has dedicated particular attention to environmentally sustainable systems that exploit passive cooling.

Finally, the roofs have been designed as hanging gardens, with palm groves that will create an urban garden to contrast with the surrounding skyscrapers when viewed from above, moderating the impact of the bulk and mass of the complex. L.D.

282 top The Cliffscrapers reintroduce the verticality of the skycraper but on a smaller scale. These structures will descend into the valleys while clinging to the mountain's slope. Cantilevered structures emphasize the thought-provoking effect of their composition.

282-283 The Units is a conglomeration of residences built in cube structures, arranged over the downward slope of the mountain, repeating the cubic shape as if they were pixels in a computer image.

283 This aerial image shows the entire resort complex, highlighting its structure from a distance as it unwinds among the undulations of the mountain chain that separates Ras Al Khaimah from Oman.

Rak Jebel al Jais Mountain Resort

DUBAI

The Rak Jebel al Jais Mountain Resort is a planned holiday resort in the mountains of the emirate of Ras Al Khaimah. It has been designed by OMA for Rakeen Development and consists of hotels, villas and apartments, offices, cafés and restaurants, commercial areas, and a conference and exhibition center. The emergence of a new kind of adventure tourism, featuring exploration holidays and survival trails in natural environments, appears to justify the creation of this new complex, whose function is not otherwise any different from that of other projects underway for the expansion of the UAE's cities.

The attraction of Rak Jebel al Jais lies in its setting: a bare, inaccessible, semi-lunar landscape, in the wild mountains dividing Ras Al Khaimah from neighboring Oman. OMA's project is aimed at valorizing the barren, rugged scenery of the area instead of taming it with contrived artificial landscaping or the construction of architectural interpretations of a supposed local tradition, so typical of many resorts.

The resort will be laid out along a 6.2-mile (10-km) course that follows the ridge, like a linear city, creating a tourist "trail" that links a series of observation points with stunning views over the surrounding area. The buildings, consisting of regular geometric shapes such as cubes and parallelepipeds, or abstract shapes representing rock formations, will be emphasized by bright colors and contrast with the natural surroundings without altering the integrity of the landscape. In many cases the outer skin, designed to shade the buildings, reinterprets the characteristic intricate geometric patterns of Islamic figurative art. The structures will be grouped together with varying densities to explore a variety of possible urban solutions for mountain living.

Villas will be regularly spaced along the length of the new Jebel al Jais Road, enjoying unobstructed views over the valleys. Their gardens will be incorporated into the floor plans to avoid the uncontrolled transformation of the rugged land on which they stand. The line of these Modern Villas will be broken by ten different developments, which will emphasize the natural beauty of the mountains. The first of these is known as the Terraces and will feature a stepped configuration in which apartments are alternated with outdoor pools, cafés, and patios, which will extend to comprise private gardens and public areas on the flat roofs of the floor below. The Wedge will be a single structure modeled like an extension of the mountain, and its terraced roof will create a plaza that can be used as an outdoor movie theater or a performance venue. Below, a ramp will descend through the building, connecting the plaza to the fluid internal space that will house a hotel, apartments, a community center, commercial areas, and a cable car terminus at the bottom.

The Outcrop will consist of a series of courtyard buildings embedded in the slope in a seemingly haphazard arrangement that optimizes view angles and the vertical connections between the levels. The courtyards will feature gardens and sports facilities, cafés, and pools. Like a pixelated carpet over the landscape, the Units development will form a collection of small cubes that create a kind of geometric abstraction of the natural terrain on which they are sited. Together with Cliff City, the development will form a dense urban zone at the highest point of the site, which will descend over the crest of the mountain and be crossed by a maze of narrow alleys running between the residential units and commercial areas. The Cliffscrapers will be a series of inverted skyscrapers that cling to the mountainside, dropping down to anchor into the cliff below and creating panoramic plazas on the roofs. The Bridge and the Dam are residential developments that will connect the walls of a gully and a valley, which are crossed by the unbroken tourist "trail." Jutting out of the mountain, the Cantilever will be the gateway to the resort and will house a cable car station. Lastly, the Suspension Unit villas will be suspended over a sheer drop accessible by elevators and cable cars.   L.D.

284-285 The Bridge is a
structure that connects the two
sides of a valley like a bridge.
In its interior, the route
connecting the building's
different complexes continues
onto one of the intermediate
levels where sports facilities
and public spaces are situated.

285 top The Wedge is a block
where a terminal connecting
various cablecar routes is
housed. Inside, a ramp links the
various functional zones which
have an essentially public
character.

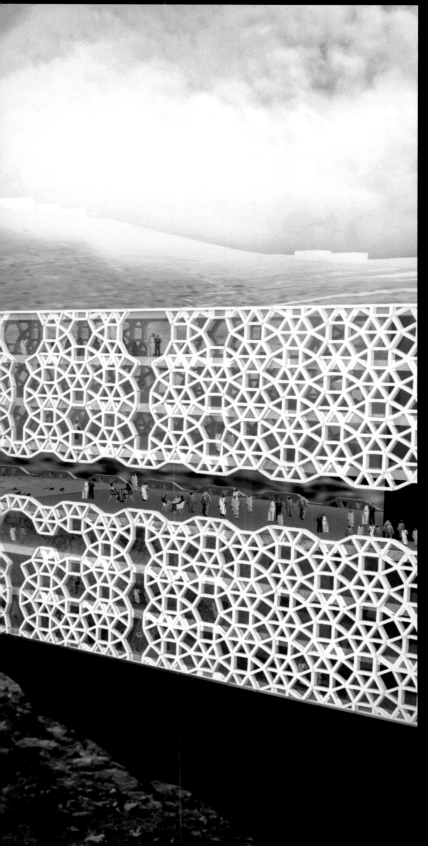

285 center The Outcrop is constructed from an ensemble of courtyard buildings, and will include areas for sports and gardening activities. Its design guarantees superb panoramic views for all of the apartments.

285 bottom The Dam takes the imposing form of a dam without its practical function, instead it will have residential spaces on numerous levels.

The Gateway

RAS AL KHAIMAH

The Gateway is a mixed-use complex designed by Dutch architecture firm OMA that will form the emblematic entrance to Gateway City, the planned new urban development that will enlarge the capital of the emirate of Ras Al Khaimah, which is about 100 miles (160 km) east of Dubai. The project was commissioned by the Ras Al Khaimah Investment Authority and property developer Rakeen from Norwegian architectural firm Snøhetta, which recently made international headlines with its design for the Bibliotheca Alexandrina in Egypt.

The complex will house several four- and five-star hotels, a conference and exhibition center, and commercial spaces with a total covered area of around 3 million sq ft (278,000 sq m). Still at the development stage, the project will also feature the landscaping of open spaces and gardens, for a total area of more than 4.8 million sq ft (445,000 sq m). The building will be set in the vast space of the desert of the Arabian Peninsula, interpreting the form of the nearby mountains with its minimalist abstract forms. Its structures will be "dematerialized" by the superimposition of slightly undulating white surfaces whose walls and roofs will merge seamlessly and rise upwards to form the tower, creating a distinctive landmark evoking a rearing cobra. The modulated surfaces will enfold the habitable horizontal planes, which will be set back to create a variety of shaded areas and to protect the interiors from excessive solar gain. The structure will be perforated by wide circular openings forming public plazas with palm trees on the ground level and terraces with private hanging gardens on the top floor. Existing roads and a raised monorail will connect the complex to the new adjoining structure. The 656-ft (200-m) tall skyscraper will house a luxury five-star hotel, whose suites will have panoramic views over the Persian Gulf, the mountains, and the capital.

Local firm Ras Al Khaimah Ceramics, the world leader in the production of ceramics for the construction industry, will be involved in the development of special white panels to clad the entire complex. The various modules have a unique irregular four-sided shape, which allows them to follow the curved profile of the skin, and will be arranged to form a complex geometric pattern recalling the decorative motifs of Islamic architecture.   L.D.

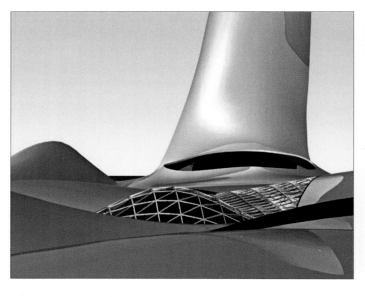

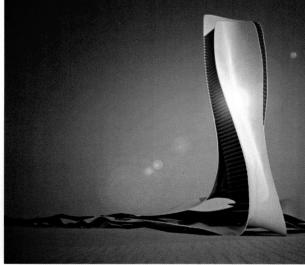

286 left For this structure's external materials, special panels were developed in collaboration with a local firm, Ras Al Khaimah Ceramics, the worldwide leader in the ceramics industry.

286 right Vaguely reminiscent of a cobra ready to attack, the tower rises to a central position in relation to the other low-rise structures, assuming a central role in the development of this area, even at a distance.

286-287 This architectural proposal is characterized by the superimposition of white abstract surfaces, among which habitable floors have been created and stepped back to avoid direct sunlight.

287 top Circular patios on many levels will bring light and air into the interior spaces and they will have public gardens and private terraces with trees. The complex will also feature other landscaped open spaces.

288-289 This complex is located in the desert outside of more densely populated areas, creating a point of access connected via a new road and a railroad.

290-291 The Crescent's buildings are autonomous but linked via the lower floors. The low-rise buildings are in the background, with enclosures in green tones, as well as the skyscrapers that complete this proposed development.

290 bottom This vertical section of the Crescent buildings shows how the concept was developed from truncated pyramids with a common lower level. Their geometry proves more linear with respect to the skyscrapers that are entrusted with the iconic role in this project.

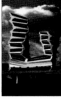

Marina Dubai
DUBAI

This project was designed by the Mexican architecture firm Rojkind Arquitectos in association with the Office for Urbanism and was the winning entry of the competition held in 2007 by Ajman Freezone Development for the master plan of Dubai Marina. The coastal development features residential buildings, offices, and commercial spaces. Rojkind's concept is based on a combination of high-rise and low-rise buildings, which gives the complex its distinctive identity. The development has a tripartite structure with two almost symmetrical parts, each composed of a pair of tall buildings surrounded by low-rise ones and flanked by a semicircular section facing the sea.

The design of the complex is based on an irregular grid of broken lines, in both the plan and the elevation. The culmination of this theme is realized in the two pairs of skyscrapers connected at ground level by a shared podium located in a prime position, and which will constitute the focal point of the complex. The geometric structure of these buildings, 33 and 23 stories tall, appears to be altered by a quavering movement evoked by split and jagged volumes, in both the plan and the section, with an effect reminiscent of coral formations.

291 bottom This cross section of the Crescent shows the designated functions of various levels, with commercial space on the ground floor, opening onto exterior public areas and a central courtyard, both used for relaxation.

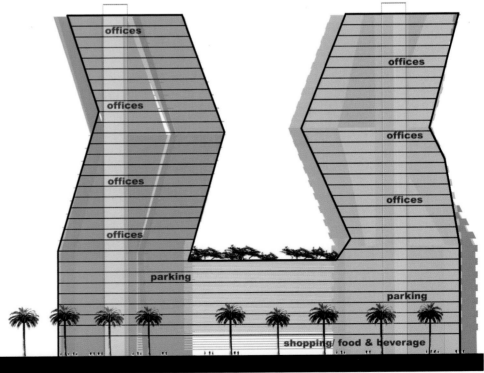

292-293 In the foreground,
you can see the offices that
emerge from the lower level
of commercial spaces and the
skyscrapers in the background.
The whole complex faces onto
a coastal promenade with access
to piers and docking facilities for
pleasure craft.

292 bottom The tall buildings
represent an architectural symbol
that gives identity to the project,
thanks to the complex geometry
of these spaces, which
emphasizes their elevation and
reflect light onto the water.

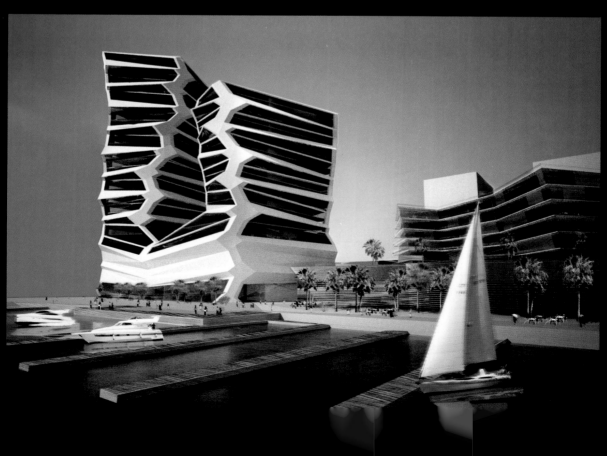

Marina Dubaï

The distinctive morphology of the towers, intended to evoke the dynamism of light reflected off water, is achieved by means of a central core housing elevator shafts and stairwells and an external white framework that is clearly visible on the façade. The structural system is designed naturally without an orthogonal grid and reinforces the irregular corners where the surfaces of the glazed façades meet. This allows the creation of free floor plans, maximizing the flexibility of the interiors.

The low-rise buildings are more integrated with the design of the open spaces. They have zigzagging floor plans, and will stand on a large podium housing commercial spaces and whose jagged lines recall a stylized rocky coast. This podium will overlook a tree-lined promenade. Its roof will have a larger open area, planted with palm trees, forming a sort of public plaza. The pedestrian accessibility and visual openness of the area will be ensured by a system of paths crossing it at ground level. This will multiply the length of the store windows,

consequently increasing the commercial value of the spaces.

The comb-shaped layout is also the design model for the organization of the areas further back. The six-story buildings taper dramatically downwards, because the floors increase in size as they go higher, while the façades lean forward. Green brises-soleils and large overhanging terraces protect the glazed surfaces from the sun, and the design of the elevations is highly graphical. This combination of high- and low-rise buildings is juxtaposed with the crescent, which will also feature a podium from which independent buildings emerge. The composition of this part of the project is also based on irregular truncated pyramidal structures, but with simpler lines. The shape of each of them is treated in a different manner, but the overall effect is well integrated and highly sculptural. Visual and functional unity is imparted by the podium, which will create a hierarchical system of public spaces by connecting the waterfront to an inner courtyard.   L.D.

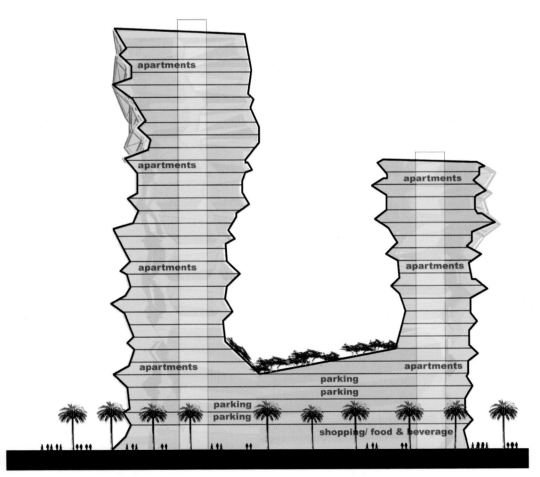

293 top These skyscrapers are linked in pairs through a common lower level that is partly empty apart from housing other facilities such as parking.

293 bottom Clearly evident in this section is the course of the façades, relying upon irregular broken lines, and the supporting function of the central services core. All floors are free of structural obstructions, guaranteeing maximum flexibility in their use.

Masdar Development

ABU DHABI

Paradoxically, it was the government of one of the world's leading petroleum-producing nations that, in April 2006, launched an international cooperation program for research into alternative energy sources and their promotion and sustainable development. This fundamental step will ensure Abu Dhabi a prominent role in the quest for solutions to humanity's most pressing problems, from the exhaustion of natural resources to climate change. Some of the world's leading companies, educational institutions, and investors are involved in the Masdar Initiative (*masdar* is the Arabic word for "source"), headed by the Abu Dhabi Future Energy Company (ADFEC). One of the first projects is Masdar City, a planned city covering an area of 2.3 sq miles (6 sq km) and home to 50,000 people. The city will contain residential areas (30% of the city), commercial areas (13%), a university (6%), public and cultural buildings (9%), transport infrastructure (8%), and a Special Economic Zone for companies involved in the production and development of low-energy impact technologies (24%). The city will also be home to the ADFEC headquarters, a center for the innovation, promotion, and commercialization of sustainable technologies.

The program offers unique opportunities for the creation of synergies between academic research and the commercial world through a well-structured policy of incentives and concessions for almost 1,500 companies. The model community, with zero emissions and zero fossil-fuel consumption, will utilize and trial innovations and models for sustainable development in various fields, ranging from construction to transport, biodiversity, and waste recycling. The city's master plan was entrusted to the British architecture firm Foster + Partners, which has combined traditional settlement solutions with the very latest technologies. The square plan features a rigid orthogonal grid, broken only by the curving line of the railway and the vegetation that cuts diagonally through it. The project takes the form of a high-density walled city, typical of traditional Islamic urban planning, which is protected from excessive solar radiation by its compact buildings, separated by narrow streets. Where necessary, in squares and wide streets, the open spaces will be shaded by canopies and screens. The geometric patterns of the shutters and the outer cladding of the buildings are characterized by tiny or oversized arabesques, reinterpreted in modern materials to establish cultural continuity with their setting.

Cars will be banned from the city, which is designed for pedestrian access only and will be served by an extensive track-based public transport network, where users are never more than 650 ft (200 m) from a stop. The airport and central Abu Dhabi can be reached by both a new light railway and existing roads. The project will be built in two stages, commencing with a huge 40-megawatt system of solar cells, which will subsequently power the construction of the city

294 This scale model's view from above emphasizes the dense fabric and regularity of the orthogonal orientation of this newly established city surrounded by a wall.

294-295 From a bird's-eye view, this 3D simulation represents the entire city and, at left of the background, you can get a glimpse of the hundreds of wind turbines that provide an alternative energy source.

295 bottom The model represents the distribution of spaces and the orthogonal road network in different colors, broken up by open areas and the curvilinear lines of the public transportation network.

itself. The city has been conceived to be almost self-sufficient in terms of both energy and other resources. Outside the perimeter of the complex the solar panels will be flanked by a wind farm; a desalination plant and a wastewater treatment plant; the experimental cultivation of food crops and plantations of various plant species for the production of biofuel; and leisure and tourist facilities.

Particular attention is paid to recycling waste – up to 99% of the total amount – by reuse, composting, and incineration with energy recovery. Other more economic alternative energy sources include thermodynamic solar technologies, featuring a system of parabolic mirrors to heat water for domestic use or to transform it into steam to power electric turbines. Geothermal heat pumps exploit the lower temperature of the subsoil in relation to the external air to cool the buildings with energy savings of up to 50 percent.   L.D.

297 top The square and streets are protected from excessive solar radiation by these shading devices that recapture and reinterpret Islamic decorative architecture in an abstract geometrical design.

296-297 Water and vegetation are skillfully utilized to passively control the microclimate of open spaces, making them livable despite the extreme temperatures in this region.

297 bottom The electric public transportation network is organized in such a way that the maximum distance travelled on foot to reach any stop is no more than 656 ft (200 m).

298-299 Extremely well designed open spaces is one of the primary objectives of this urban settlement, which has the aim of providing exclusive accessibility for pedestrian thoroughfares and public transport.

299 top This construction proposal makes explicit reference to the dense urban fabric of the traditional Islamic city where the proximity of buildings contributes to shielding the environs from direct sunlight.

299 center In the city, a number of public agencies and organizations have found an appropriate site for research and development, among which is the Masdar Institute for Science and Technology.

299 bottom Awnings with geometric cutouts project evocative chiaroscuro effects on the buildings and sidewalks outside, enriching the quality of these open spaces.

AUTHORS

OSCAR EUGENIO BELLINI, born in 1965, is an architect and researcher at the Building Environment Science & Technology Department of the Politecnico di Milano. As a researcher he focuses on project-related themes addressing the relationship between technology and the constructability of architecture. In addition to his research activity he participates in national and international architecture competitions. Author of *Free Parcels, un'innovazione tipologica al quartiere Borneo Sporenburg* (Maggioli Editore, 2007), he collaborated on various publications, among which L'intervento sul costruito. *Problemi e orientamenti* (Edizioni Franco Angeli, 2002).

LAURA DAGLIO, who was born in 1970, is an architect. She teaches architectural technology at the Faculty of Architecture and Society at the Politecnico di Milano, where she is a researcher in the Building Environment Science & Technology Department. A contributor to various magazines, she is one of the authors of *Tecnologie per l'igiene edilizia e ambientale* (CLUP, 2002) and of *Edificio, salute e ambiente. Tecnologie sostenibili per l'igiene edilizia e ambientale* (Hoepli, 2007). She took part in the realizing of *La casa popolare in Lombardia: 1903-2003*, an exhibition that took place at the 2005 Triennale di Milano.

BIBLIOGRAPHY

BOOKS:

Alvin Boyarsky, Joseph Giovannini, Detlef Mertins and Patrick Schumacher, *Zaha Hadid: Thirty Years of Architecture*, Guggenheim Museum Publications, New York 2006.

Sabina Marreiros (ed.), *Dubai: Architecture & Design*, Daab, Köln 2006.

Philip Jodidio, *Architecture in the Emirates*, Taschen, Köln 2007.

Al Abed Ibraim, Paula Vine, Peter Hellyer and Peter Vine, *United Arab*

Emirates Yearbook 2008, Trident Press Ltd., London 2008.

MAGAZINES (in chronological order):

John E. Czarnecki, "SOM designs world's tallest tower for Dubai developer", *Architectural Record*, July 2003, v. 191, n. 7, page 30.

Andres Lepik, "Searching for the limits: 'the building type skyscraper at the beginning of the 21st century'", *A + U: architecture and urbanism*, October 2005, n. 10 (421), pages 16-25.

Sebastiano Brandolini, "Dubai città

miraggio", *Ottagono*, april 2007, n. 199, pages 164-210.

Chris Bosse, "The injection of building culture into the construction boom: new architecture in Dubai", *A + U: architecture and urbanism*, May 2007, n. 5 (440), pages 86-95.

"Snøhetta Architects: the Gateway Project, Ras Al Khaimah", *Arca*, July-August 2007, n. 227, pages 48-49.

"Infinity-David Fisher Architects: Rotating Tower, Dubai", *Arca*, July-August 2007, n. 227, pages 52-57.

INDEX

PHOTO CREDITS

AISA: pages 2-3
Marla Anderson/Alamy: page 68
ArabianEye/Contrasto: pages 31, 179 top, 180-181, 184 top
Arco Images GmbH/Alamy: page 165 top
Patrik Beckers/FabPics: pages 25, 67
Walter Bibikow/Corbis: page 242
Georgina Bowater/Corbis: page 178 right
Peter Bowater/Alamy: page 70
Charles Bowman/Alamy: page 33
Victor S. Brigola/artur: page 178 left
Charles Crowell/Bloomberg/Getty Images: page 117
Ian Cumming/Getty Images: page 183
Deco/Alamy: page 164
Etienne De Malglaive/Gamma Eyedea Presse/Eyedea/Contrasto: pages 243 top, 243 bottom
Neil Emmerson/Getty Images: pages 106-107
epa/Corbis: page 179 bottom
H.G. Esch: pages 18-19, 78, 79, 80 top, 80 bottom, 81, 82, 83
Keith Erskine/Alamy: page 186
EifelGary/Alamy: page 161
George Hammerstein/Solus-Veer/Corbis: page 187

Dominic Harrison/Alamy: page 167
Hufton+Crow/VIEW: pages 71, 73, 236 bottom, 237, 238-239, 239 top, 239 bottom, 240, 240-241, 255, 257
Chris Jackson/Getty Images: pages 116, 242-243, 244-245
Stephanie Kuykendal/Corbis: pages 244, 245 top
Holger Leue/Lonely Planet Images: pages 110-111
Emile Luider/Eyedea/Contrasto: pages 185, 188-189
Bill Lyons/Alamy: page 166
Richard Manin/HOA-QUI/Eyedea/Contrasto: page 304
Angus McComiskey/Alamy: pages 162-163
Greg Newington/Photolibrary Group: page 8-9
Jock Pottle of Esto Photographics: pages 44 left, 46 top
Philippe Renault/Gamma/Contrasto: page 184 bottom
Philippe Renault/Hemis/Corbis: page 66
Christopher Roberts/ Axiomphotographic.com: pages 164-165

Hugh Sitton/Getty Images: page 176
David Steele/Getty Images: pages 76-77
Paul Thuysbaert/Photolibrary Group: pages 182-183
VIEW Pictures Ltd/Alamy: pages 254 left, 254 right, 256
Beth Wald/Getty Images: page 245 bottom
Peter Widmann/Alamy: page 165 bottom
Jeremy Woodhouse/Masterfile/Sie: pages 105, 176-177
Courtesy of Aedas Ltd: pages 15, 36, 37, 38, 39, 40-41, 41, 42, 43
Courtesy of Al Nakheel Properties: pages 266-267, 268 top right, 268 center, 268 bottom, 268-269, 269, 270-271, 271, 272 top, 272 bottom, 273, 274 top, 274 bottom, 274-275, 276, 276-277, 277 top, 277 bottom
Courtesy of Carlos Ott Architect: page 69
Courtesy of Arkan Architects-Consultants: pages 160 top, 160 bottom, 162
Courtesy of Ateliers Jean Nouvel: pages 190, 190-191, 191 top, 191 bottom, 192, 192-193, 193, 194 top, 194 bottom, 194-195, 216-217, 218-219, 219, 220, 220-221, 221 top, 221 bottom

Courtesy of WS Atkins & Partners: pages 24, 26 left, 26 right, 27 top, 27 bottom, 289, 29, 30 top, 30 bottom, 88 top, 88 bottom, 89, 90 left, 90 right, 91, 260-261, 261

Courtesy of Asymptote – Hani Rashid + Lise Anne Couture: pages 228, 228-229, 229, 230, 230-231, 231

Courtesy of Jung Brannen Associates: pages 84, 85, 86, 87

Courtesy of Dynamic Architecture: pages 11, 54-55, 55, 56, 57 top left, 57 center, 57 right, 58, 59 top, 59 bottom left, 59 bottom right, 60 top, 60 bottom, 60-61

Courtesy of Foster + Partners: pages 118 left, 118 right, 119 top, 119 bottom, 120, 121, 278, 279 top, 279 bottom, 280-281, 294, 294-295, 295, 296-297, 297 top, 297 bottom, 298-299, 299 top, 299 center, 299 bottom

Courtesy of Gehry Partners LLP: pages 212 top, 212-213 top and bottom, 214-215

Courtesy of Gensler: pages 72-73, 74, 75

Courtesy of Glenn Howells - 360TimeWorld (for further information, visit the website at www.360timeworld.com, write to info@360TimeWorld.com, or call 0044 7779 360 360): pages 48, 49, 50-51, 52, 52-53, 53

Courtesy of Hufton & Crow – Hok Hellmuth, Obata & Kassabaum: pages 236 top, 241

Courtesy of Jumeirah Properties: pages 6-7, 104, 108, 109 top, 109 bottom, 112, 113 top, 113 center, 113 bottom, 114, 115pages 168 top, 168 center, 168

bottom, 168-169, 170-171, 172 top, 172 bottom, 172-173, 174-175

Courtesy of Rojkind Arquitectos: pages 290, 290-291, 291, 292, 292-293, 293 top, 293 bottom

Courtesy of Kohn Pedersen Fox Associates: pages 76 top, 76 bottom, 77 bottom

Courtesy of Llewelyn Davies Yeang in association with T.R.Hamzah & Yeang Sdn. Bhd.: pages 138, 138-139, 139, 140, 140-141, 141

Courtesy of OMA: pages 12-13, 126-127, 128-129, 130, 131, 282, 282-283, 283, 284-285, 285 top, 285 center, 285 bottom

Courtesy of RMJM: pages 32-33, 34-35

Courtesy of RUR Architecture: pages 92-93, 93, 94-95, 96-97, 9798, 98-99, 99

Courtesy of Sanjay Puri Architects Pvt Ltd: pages 200-201, 201 left, 201 right, 202 top, 202 bottom, 202-203

Courtesy of SOM (Skidmore, Owings & Merrill LLP): pages 44 right, 45, 46 bottom, 47, 122 top, 122 bottom, 123 (PMB Design), 124-125 (PMB Design), 125

Courtesy of Snøhetta AS: pages 286 left, 286 right, 286-287, 287, 288-289

Courtesy of Sybarite: pages 1, 142, 143, 144, 145, 196 top, 196 bottom, 197 top, 197 center, 197 bottom, 198-199, 199 top, 199 center, 199 bottom

Courtesy of Tadao Ando Architects and Associates: pages 10, 208-209 210, 210-211

Courtesy of TDCI Tourism Development & Investment Company: pages 206-207, 207

Courtesy of gmp Architekten von Gerkan, Marg und Partner: pages 246-247, 247 left, 247 right, 248, 248-249, 249

Courtesy of Zaha Hadid & Associates: pages 4-5, 16-17, 132, 132-133, 133, 134, 135, 136, 136-137, 146-147, 147, 148-149, 150, 150-151, 152, 153, 154-155, 155 top, 55 bottom, 222, 222-223, 223, 224, 225 top, 225 center, 225 bottom, 226, 226-227, 258-259, 259

Cover

The Burj Khalifa in Dubai, inaugurated in January 2010, is the highest skyscraper in the world.
© Charles Crowell/Bloomberg/Getty Images

Back cover

The original volumetric solution adopted by the anglo-iraqi architect Zaha Hadid for the tower known as The Opus, in the Business Bay distric of Dubai, bears witness to the innovative research that characterizes the area's new architectural style.
© Courtesy of Zaha Hadid Architects

ACKNOWLEDGMENTS

The Publisher would like to thank:

Aedas Ltd, London: Gordon Cheung, Lillian Ma and Lyndal Stuart
Al Nakheel Properties, Dubai: Aaron Richardson and Shabana Sonde
Arkan Architects-Consultants, Abu Dhabi: Abadi Arkan Al Abadi
Asymptote Architecture, New York: Heidi Druckemiller
Ateliers Jean Nouvel, Paris: Charlotte Huisman
Atkinsglobal, Cusano Milanino (Milan): Gregorio Guidobono Cavalchini
Dynamic Architecture - Rotating Tower Technology International Limited, Florence: Simona Casati
Foster + Partners, London: Kathryn Tollervey
Gehry Partners, LLP, Los Angeles: Rhiannon Gharibeh and Rachel Judlowe (Ruder Finn)
Gensler, London: Kirsten Rothey
Giffels Associates Limited, Toronto: Burt Meredig
Glenn Howells - 360TimeWorld, Dubai: Tav Singh
gmp Architekten von Gerkan, Marg und Partner, Hamburg: Bettina Ahrens
HOK Hellmuth, Obata + Kassabaum: Helen Caswell
Jan De Nul NV, Hofstade - Aalst (Belgium): Heleen Schellinck
Jung Brannen Associates: Katherine Cusack
Kohn Pedersen Fox Associates, London: Elizabeth Walker
Llewelyn Davies Yeang, London: Ken Yeang, Ting Lam Tang and Loo See Chew
NORR Group, Abu Dhabi: Yahya Jan, Christina Yesudhas and Dolphy D'Sa
Office for Metropolitan Architecture [OMA], Rotterdam: Isabel Pagel
Carlos Ott Architect, Montevideo: Sandra Rosas
RMJM Middle East, Dubai: Louise Fichera
Rojkind Arquitectos, Mexico City: Tomaz Kristof and Carlos Ortiz
RUR Architecture, New York: Neil Cook
Sanjay Puri Architects, Mumbai: Sanjay Puri and Sapna Khakaria
Snøhetta AS, Oslo: Karianne Pedersen
SOM (Skidmore, Owings & Merrill LLP), Chicago: Amy Hawkinson
SOM (Skidmore, Owings & Merrill LLP), New York: Lauren Bebry and Elizabeth Kubany
Sybarite UK Ltd, London: Tara Robertson
WS Atkins & Partners, Dubai: Katie Hodge and Maya Mary Thomas
Zaha Hadid Architects, London: Davide Giordano

WS White Star Publishers® is a registered trademark property of Edizioni White Star s.r.l.

© 2008, 2010 Edizioni White Star s.r.l.
Via M. Germano, 10
13100 Vercelli, Italy
www.whitestar.it

TRANSLATION:
Sarah Ponting (text)
Erin Jennison (captions)

ISBN 978-88-544-0550-9

3 4 5 6   15 14 13 12 11

Printed in Indonesia

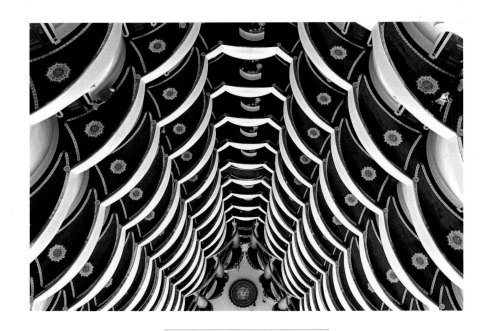

304 Inside the Burj Al Arab in
Dubai, skillfully rendered views,
use of special finish materials and
decorative elements repeated
throughout the various levels
create a surprising ambiance in
the atrium and loggia leading to
suite entrances, directing visitors'
attention towards the gushing
fountain on the ground floor.